HARTFORDE

M

20 40 60 80 100

PASES

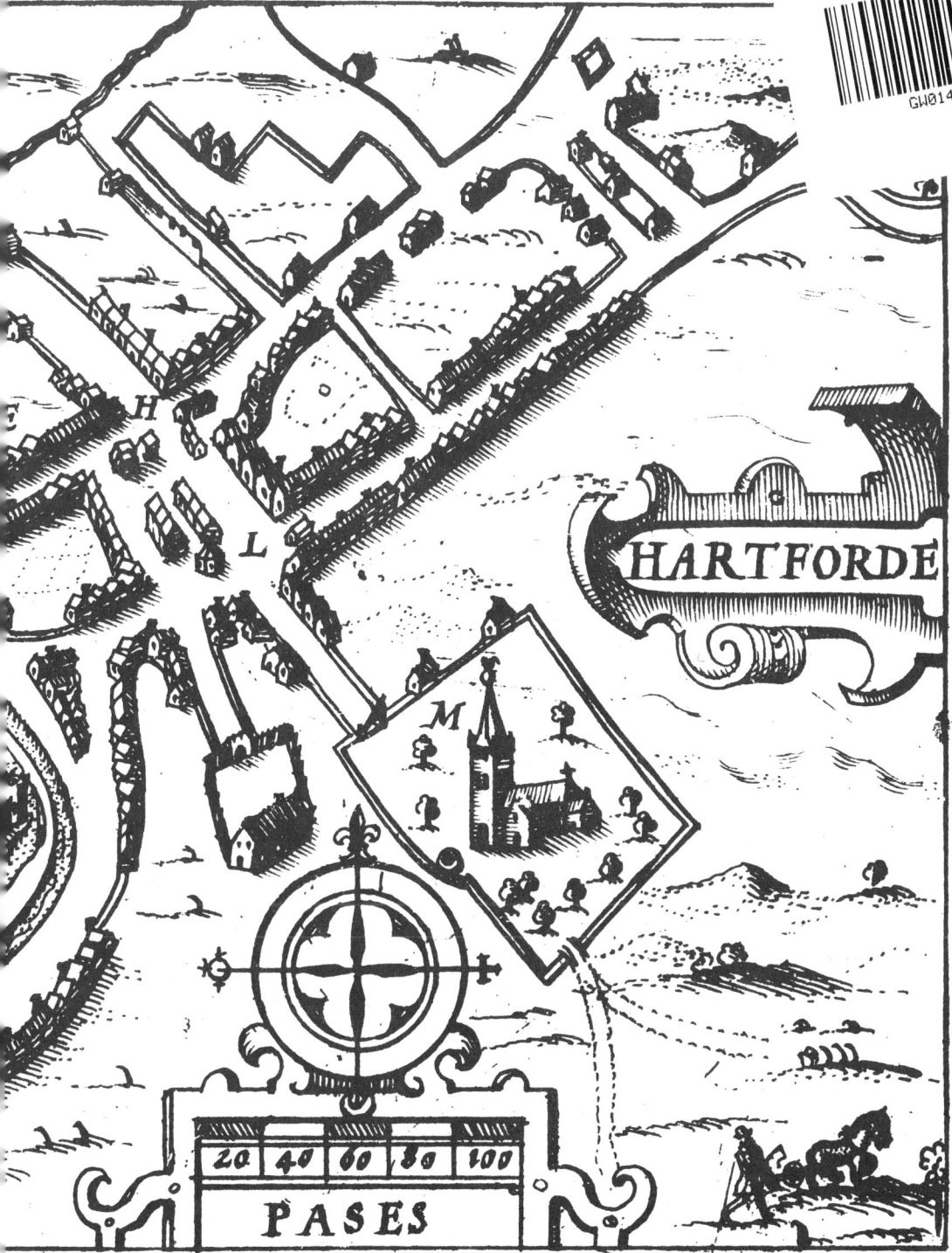

REPRODUCED BY PERMISSION OF HERTFORD MUSEUM.

...re it was demolished early in the 17th century. It is also the
...Church of St. Nicholas.

THE BOOK OF HERTFORD

THE NORTH PROSPECT OF THE TOWN OF HERTFORD FROM PORTHILL

Drapentier's view of Hertford from Port Hill in 1691. This engraving by a Frenchman cost the corporation £3/15/0.

THE BOOK OF HERTFORD

THE STORY OF THE TOWN
BY

CYRIL HEATH

BARON

MCMXCII

FIRST PUBLISHED IN 1975, IN A SECOND EDITION IN 1987
AND IN THIS SECOND IMPRESSION IN 1992
BY BARON BIRCH FOR QUOTES LIMITED, WHITTLEBURY, NORTHANTS
AND PRODUCED BY KEY COMPOSITION, SOUTH MIDLANDS LITHOPLATES,
CHENEY & SONS, HILLMAN PRINTERS (FROME) LIMITED
AND WBC BOOKBINDERS.

© CYRIL HEATH 1975 & 1987
DOROTHY HEATH 1992

ISBN 0 86023 402 9

Contents

Acknowledgements 8
Foreword by the Marquess of Salisbury 9
Preface by Councillor Mrs Joan Coleman 9
Hartford 10
Introduction: Pride in our past 11

Hertford-on-Thames 12
The Synod of 673 19
Danish Riddle 23
Castle and Kings 32
Royal Prison 40
Regal Retreat 46
The Church 54
Great Houses 66
Markets and Mills 76
Law and Disorder 88
The Gain of Learning 106
Into Battle 114
A Peal of People 124

Epilogue: Faith in our Future 141
Appendix: Full list of canons passed by the Synod of Hertford 144
Bibliography 144
Index 145

Acknowledgements

The Beatles once had a song called "I get by with a little help from my friends." This book was produced with a lot of help from a lot of friends both old and new.

It would have been impossible but for the assistance of Gordon Davies, curator of Hertford Museum, and his staff. A fellow Welshman, Gordon has spent a lot of time and effort on my behalf.

Miss Lorna Paulin, the County Librarian, has been an inspiration from the start, and the book has received tremendous help from the town branch of the library, which held the reservation facility.

The Mayor of Hertford, Mrs. Joan Coleman, and her husband have always supported the enterprise, and Mr. Coleman gave the book a window display at his Railway Street shop.

Assistance came from the County Archives, where Miss Eileen Lynch read through the manuscript, and Miss Ann Pegrum made useful suggestions.

Gordon Moodey, for many years secretary of the East Herts Archaeological Society, also read the manuscript.

The majority of the photographs are by a colleague, Mike Poultney, who put himself out to complete the work on time.

The picture of Princess Elizabeth at the age of 12, by an unknown artist, is reproduced by gracious permission of Her Majesty the Queen.

Thanks are due to Simon Houfe for permission to use the Panshanger pictures by Herbert Felton, and to Rex Wailes for the pictures of the fulling stocks, and the New River water gauge.

The cover picture is by Tony Osborne, and I am grateful to Cyril Nicholson and Raymond Wingate for helping out with a number of pictures.

Pictures by the late George Blake are published by kind permission of his widow, and those of the interior of St. Leonard's church, by permission of the Rector, the Rev. Colin Weale.

The picture of the Friends Meeting House is by Dr. W. R. M. Thompson, and it, and several details of the house are published by kind permission of Dr. Violet Rowe.

Miss Winifred Baker provided the picture of the 1915 bomb damage in Bull Plain.

To Ken Gardner many thanks for smoothing the way to the British Museum.

Dr. Paul Sangster kindly gave permission for any details I required from his booklet on Balls Park and the picture of Hertford's old gallows came from Madame Tussaud's.

Finally my wife has been a source of tremendous inspiration, and there was encouragement from Miss Inez Rossiter, who at 83 still took a lively interest in the town. (1975)

Dedication ·· For Dorothea

Foreword

by The Marquess of Salisbury

Hertford is one of the oldest inhabited places in the county. People lived there before the beginning of recorded history. Why it came into being we shall probably never know, but from the earliest times, it has been a place of importance. It was the venue for the Synod to which it gave its name, and which established the future of Christianity in this country. Later, its castle was to control the area north of London, making it the key point during the turbulence of the Middle Ages. Latterly, it has played its part as the county town, and has retained its importance to the present.

The town has also retained its character, as it nestles beneath the castle walls, although it has nonetheless moved with the times. Side by side with the ancient houses in the old streets are newer buildings, supermarkets, car parks, new schools, and standing above it, County Hall – as important now in its own way as was the castle in its heyday.

Hertford is steeped in history, and there is much to tell about its past: both about what happened here, how it grew, and about its streets and buildings. This is what this book sets out to do, and it will surely find many readers from among its own citizens, and visitors to the town.

HATFIELD HOUSE,
HATFIELD, HERTS
March, 1975

Salisbury

Preface

by Councillor Mrs Joan Coleman

To open The Book of Hertford is to open a window onto the past of which Hertfordians are so justly proud. Hertford is not one of our more important centres of trade and commerce, but the story of the town and its castle is as exciting and interesting as any. History, as portrayed by Cyril Heath, is no dull list of facts and dates, but an insight into the lives of those people, some great and some lowly, who have lived in Hertford, or have been associated with it and have contributed to the story of the county town. It is our pride in our past which gives us our faith in our future. In commending this book, I do so, confident that it will not be left to moulder on our bookshelves, but will be a constant source of interest, information and delight to all.

Joan M. Coleman

Hartford

Hartford be callid unto remembrance than
A Towne where Tearme is kept as cause doth crave,
It favoured is, and likt of each good man,
It dooth in world, itself so well behave
Gallant and gay and gladsome to the sight
Framde from the stock that still grows bolt upright
Most meeke of minde, and plain in ev'ry part
Where dutie ought show love and loyall hart

      Thomas Churchyard (1520? – 1604)
"A pleasant conceite penned in verse . . . humblie
presented on New Year's Day last to the Queens
Majestie (Elizabeth I) 1593."

The town's Coat of Arms.

Pride in our past...

Hertford boasts a glorious past. A Royal Borough for more than 1,000 years, it has seen the pomp and circumstance of regal visitors, and felt the iron boot of the savage invader.

This is not a definitive history but rather, the story of the town stripped of jargon and the Latin of royal charters; dusted off to reveal the colour and richness of the past.

Hertford was identified as the Regency town, Meryton of Jane Austin's novel "Pride and Prejudice". The Bennet's home of Longbourn is Epcombs, at Hertingfordbury; Netherfield, the home of the Bingleys, is Balls Park, and Lucas Lodge, home of Sir William and Lady Lucas, was Panshanger, or Goldings.

Much of the town's past has been carefully preserved, and this book represents a personal selection written and assembled for enjoyment as well as instruction.

The borough seal.

11

Above: Interglacial finds. Left to right: Fragment of mammoth's tooth found in Mead Lane, tooth of a woolly rhinoceros (both about 4th Ice Age), tooth of a horse, tooth of a hippopotamus (second or third interglacial period), the last three found at Waterhall Farm.

Below right: Fragment of polished flint axe head (New Stone Age) from Bengeo Common—now The Avenue.

Below left: An Old Stone Age hand axe, found in All Saints' churchyard.

Hertford-on-Thames

The River Thames once flowed through Hertford—more than a million years ago—from the Reading area to Hertford by way of St. Albans, continuing eastwards to Bishop's Stortford, and ultimately the North Sea. Then came the first of the Ice Ages, causing a glacier to form on the Chilterns, its debris carried south east, blocking the river. The Thames formed a new channel through Watford and Finchley before rejoining its old course at Ware.

The second Ice Age created a dam somewhere near Bishop's Stortford, and the Thames widened into what is known geologically as Lake Hertford, which gradually filled with debris from the dam itself: hence the flat land surface at Sele Farm, Bengeo and County Hall.

Finally a glacier moved in from the north east, sweeping right over what had been Lake Hertford, and the Thames gave up the struggle, finding its present course through London. During the interval between the second and third Ice Ages, the River Lee cut its way back from the Thames. Hippopotami sported in its waters, alongside elephants and rhinoceros. Evidence of many animals has been found in gravel pits at Water Hall Farm, near the town.

Following the third Ice Age, Early Stone Age man appeared locally, and one left his hand axe in what later became All Saints churchyard. The fourth Ice Age brought perennially cold weather to Hertford, and during the summer thaw, debris moved downhill slowly but surely. When the Castle street subway was excavated for the relief road, three river channels were discovered, each in turn filled by chalk and clay from those far off summers.

Animals aplenty thrived: mammoth, woolly rhinoceros, horse, elk, deer and early cattle all foraged where now the town stands. When the glaciers receded finally, some 12,000 years ago, the basic shape of the town's site had crystallised. As Britain ceased to be part of Europe with the melting ice cap creating the Channel 7,000 years back, the River Lee and its tributaries flowed more slowly, and their valleys became marshy, as Kings Meads still witnesses.

Flints and sometimes the remains of slain animals from those times, show man was active here. Neolithic or New Stone Age man's flint implements for hunting smaller mammals have been found north of the town.

Then the land was covered by forest, particularly dense to the south of Hertford—and in this eastern part of the county, man has left only isolated evidence of his passing. Nearly 4,000 years ago, the Beaker Folk left behind a vessel—at Ware—and Bronze Age man buried his dead at Cromwell road, Hertford, where an urn has been found. Some traces of this early settlement remain.

But the earlier New Stone Age saw farming of a primitive 'slash and burn' variety, contemporary with the building of Stonehenge. These local farmers traded countrywide, for a Lake District stone axe was dropped here by one passing trader.

With the discovery of copper, bronze and later iron, implements improved, and with them breeding of domestic stock, and crops; life became more settled, and with the arrival of the Belgae in the last century BC, came the first coinage. A gold coin was left by one at Rush Green; a lidded bowl, evidence of wheel-made pottery, has survived the intervening centuries at Queens Hill, Hertford.

For the Belgae this area was important. To the east was the tribal capital of the Trinovantes at Colchester; to the west the Cantuvellauni at St. Albans. Between the two lay the major settlement of Braughing, which was occupied by both in turn.

No evidence of Belgic occupation appeared at Hertford itself, until last year Foxholes Farm yielded proof of a ditched settlement, with traces of huts. Significantly, a shaft furnace was discovered—only the third such found in Britain—and hand made pottery, which appears to be earlier than the more normal wheel-made variety introduced about 30 BC. The settlement was probably abandoned about 50 AD, soon after the Roman conquest, but was reoccupied during the fourth century AD.

The Romans in 43 AD introduced new technology and road building. One of their most important routes was Ermine Street, which joined London to York, passing through Ware and Braughing. Hertford may not have been occupied by Romans or Romano-British, but a large number of coins found in the moat at Brickendonbury (stolen from the Museum in 1963) suggest a trading post.

The Romans certainly buried their dead at Mangrove road, and left pottery behind in Ware road. Tiles and a few fragments of pottery were found in the vicinity of The Wash.

The most significant Roman find was at Foxholes, when a Roman corn drier was discovered during the gravel winning.

The fourth century device was lifted almost intact out of the ground, restored, and is now in Hertford Museum Annexe.

After the Romans left, the Saxons penetrated the north of the county in the late 5th century AD, and re-established themselves later in the following century. It was then that the Hertingfordbury and Bengeo settlements were founded.

So by the seventh century, with England divided into seven tribal kingdoms, each with its own king and six with their own bishops, the resulting religious disunity really put Hertford squarely on the map of history for the first time—in 673 AD.

These three late Iron Age pots came from Foxholes.

14

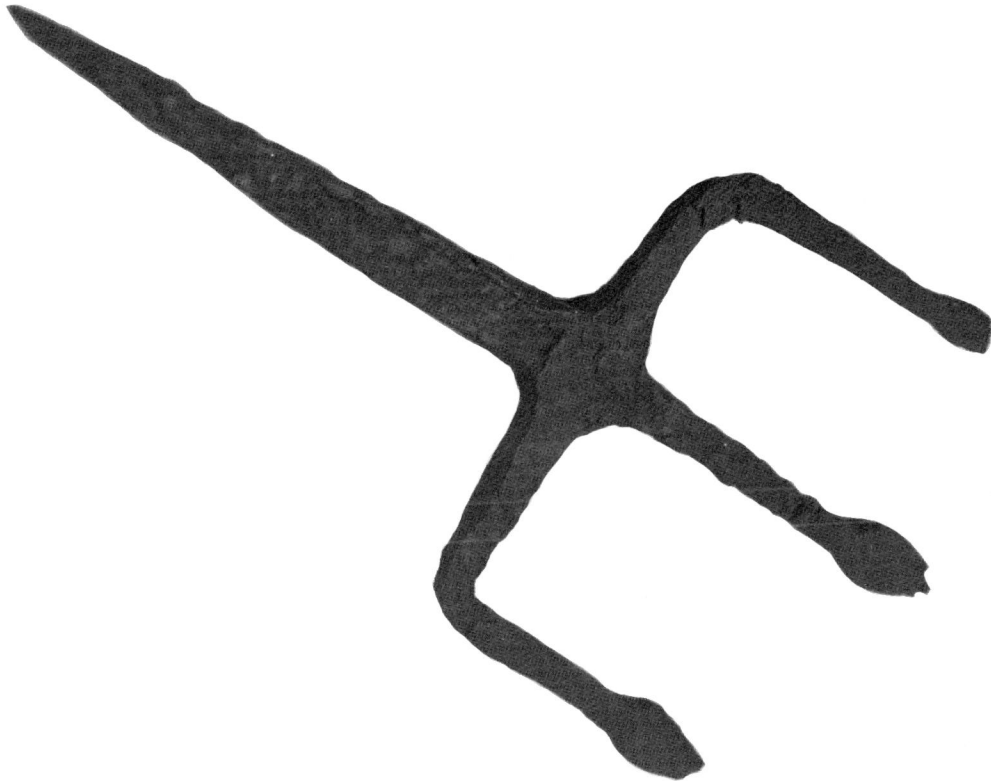

Above: Gold coin from Belgic Gaul, *c*. 100 BC, found at Rush Green.

Below: From the Foxholes dig came this fork, probably 1st century BC.

Above: Belgic bowl with lid from Queen's Hill, *c.* 30 BC-*c.* 43 AD.
The find with others in the same area, led to the 1974 Foxholes finds.

Below: Some of the 430 Roman coins which made up the Brickendonbury hoard
found in 1893. In all there were 25 different types, all of the third century.

16

Above: Late Roman pottery from Mangrove Hall. Probably a burial group.

Below: A Roman key of the third century, from Foxholes.

The first mention of Hertford in print. A page from the Venerable Bede's "History of the English Church and People", telling of the Synod of Hertford 673. The town's name is the last word on the 10th line of the second column.

The Synod of 673

There are two stones in the town which tell how in AD 673, (one does say 672), Theodore of Tarsus, then Primate of All England, called together the English bishops at Herutford—as Bede called it. The meeting of the five bishops and their clergy in the town has been described as an epoch in the history of church and nation.

Friedrich Heer, in his "Intellectual History of Europe" wrote: "The synod was the great unifying factor in England. The religious union prepared the political unity . . . In a sense England's nationalism has been religious from the beginning."

There were two forms of Christianity in England: the Celtic churches and the Roman. One of the major differences was over the keeping of Easter. There was also a minor difference over tonsure. Both missions did establish some local churches, but they were generations from being able to provide a full parish system. Theodore of Tarsus hoped to stop all this, although a more unlikely candidate could hardly have been selected. He was a layman of 65, long past the age when it is easy to adapt to new conditions; an Asiatic unable to speak a single word of the language of the country he was to shake-up so dramatically.

He filled up vacant Sees, divided Dioceses where they seemed too large, suppressed irregularities, and on September 24th 673 presided at Hertford over the first National Synod of the English Church.

Apart from Theodore, the assembly included Bisi, Bishop of the East Angles; Wilfrid, Bishop of the Northumbrians—who was represented by two proxies; Putta, Bishop of Rochester; Leutherius, Bishop of the West Saxons, and Wynfrid, Bishop of Mercia, as well as teachers, scholars, and priests. They agreed on 10 canons, which to a large extent still form the basis of the Church of England. They settled the question of Easter; stopped bishops going into other dioceses, and stopped them interfering with the monasteries. They also laid down some basic rules on marriage.

The two memorial stones perpetuate a controversy. The Bishop of St. Albans, the Rt. Rev. Michael Furze, speaking at Hertford on May 8th, 1934, suggested the Synod should be commemorated and Ald. Alex Purkiss Ginn wrote a letter to the Hertfordshire Mercury on May 18th, asking for contributions towards a memorial stone.

In the same issue Dr. Ernest C. Messenger wrote, hoping the memorial would be "in a religious edifice which is still in commune with the apostolic see which sent Theodore here and to whose authority Theodore himself appealed at the Synod," (ie: a Catholic site).

A storm of protest and counter protest dominated the local correspondence columns, until on June 13th, Dr. Messenger complained that in the wording on the stone in the Castle Grounds the Bishop of St. Albans would not allow it to be said that Theodore was appointed by the Pope in Rome.

He called for donations for a stone to be erected at the Roman Catholic Church of the

Immaculate Conception and St. Joseph in Hertford. Finally a compromise was reached by a joint statement from Alderman Purkiss Ginn and Dr. Messenger to the effect that the stone in the Castle Grounds was to be considered the civic memorial and the one at the Catholic Church the ecclesiastical one.

The stone in the Castle Grounds, of Cornish granite, was unveiled by the 4th Marquis of Salisbury, High Steward of the Borough, on October 6th, 1934. The ecclesiastical memorial in the form of an Anglo-Saxon cross, was dedicated by Dr. Hinsley, Archbishop of Westminster, on September 2nd, 1935, the Sunday after the Feast of Theodore.

Whatever the differences, they did not arise in 1973 when the town celebrated the 13th centenary of the Synod. The Roman Catholic Archbishop of Westminster conducted the opening service in the Castle Grounds, with contributions by leaders of all the other denominations.

A pageant based on the history of Christianity up to 673 was staged in the Castle Grounds, and watched by Her Majesty Queen Elizabeth, the Queen Mother. The final service, on THE day, September 24th, was led by the Archbishop of Canterbury, Dr. Michael Ramsey, and again it was fully ecumenical. The whole town went en-fête for the summer with an abundance of events of which it had not seen the like for centuries.

Why was Hertford chosen for the Synod? We do not know for certain, but a number of reasons can be advanced. It was at that time on the borders of the Kingdoms of the East Saxons, Mercia, and Wessex. All three were under the influence of the strong King of Kent who could protect the visitors therefore from Wessex and Kent, and could ensure the safety of the East Angles.

Hertford was not a major centre such as London or Canterbury and therefore political jealousies could be avoided. Geographically, it was a matter of communications. The area to the north of London was a dense oak forest cut by the more open valley of the River Lee, which was marshy and difficult to cross. Yet to reach the north of England from London it was necessary to cross this river, and the ford at Hertford was the most convenient. (The Roman bridge at Ware had been destroyed when the Saxons first came). It was this ford which was to bring the town into being, but at the time of the Synod there was probably no major settlement here, but at Hertingfordbury and Bengeo.

Her Majesty Queen Elizabeth, the Queen Mother at the 1973 pageant with J. Eric David, who played Archbishop Theodore. Afterwards he said he was so confused he did not know whether to bless her, or raise his mitre!

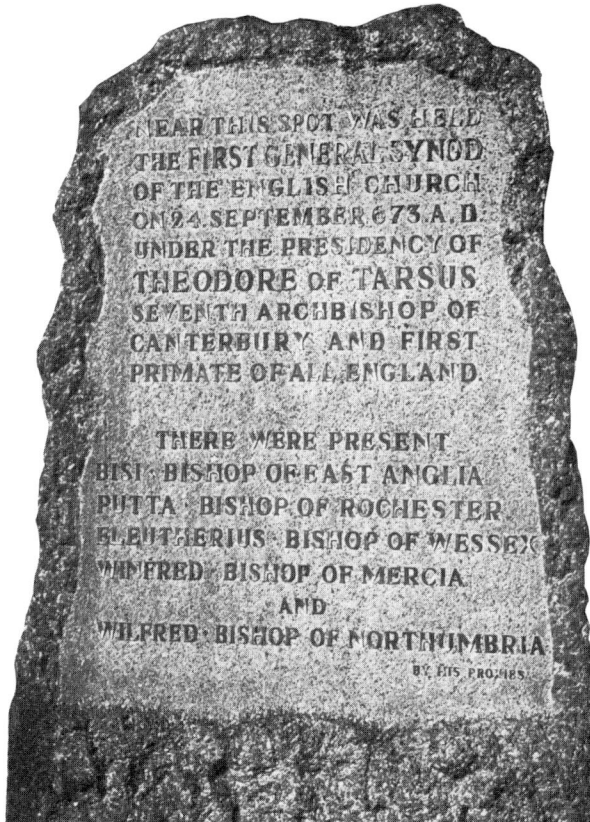

Above: Replicas of an Elizabethan chalice—one of the town's treasures—were sold for the 1300th celebrations of the synod in 1973. Chalices were given to the successor bishops. Seen here are the Bishop of St. Albans, the Rt. Rev. Robert Runcie (left), and the then Archbishop of Canterbury, Dr Michael Ramsey.

Below: The stone in the Castle grounds commemorating the synod.

21

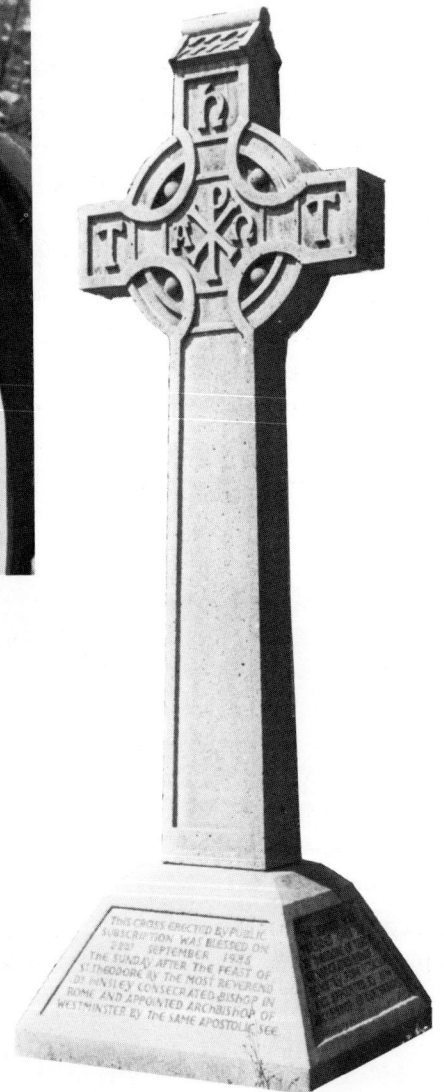

Above: The 1973 Synod celebrations were opened with a united service, at which the preacher was Cardinal Heenan (left), Roman Catholic Archbishop of Westminster. With him is the Bishop of St. Albans.

Below: The stone in the grounds of the town's Roman Catholic church.

Danish Riddle

The Kingdom of Mercia extended its boundaries eastwards in the eighth century to the line of Ermine Street, taking in Hertford and the western part of the declining Kingdom of the East Saxons. But the next significant landmark in the town's history was in 894, during the Danish invasion of England. The town was then a settlement around the ford.

The Danish invasion had been gathering momentum throughout the ninth century. The Kingdoms of the Saxons and Angles, except Wessex in the south, had been all but wiped out, and their royal families killed. By about 878 nearly half the country was in Danish hands and in that year, King Alfred of Wessex had been obliged to divide the country on the line of Watling Street. This left the land to the north in the hands of the Danish leader Guthrum, and for a while Hertford seems to have been within Danelaw.

But Alfred counter-attacked and recaptured several areas including Hertford, and the river then became the boundary from London, up the Lee, and following Watling Street to mid-Wales, then north to Cheshire. Thus we see the strategic importance of the ford. Who-ever held Hertford controlled the northern approaches to London.

Ten years later there was fresh trouble. Another powerful Danish force landed in Kent, led by a veteran Viking called Haesten. This moved into the Thames, thence up the River Lee, and the events which followed have led many historians into flights of fancy. Their favourite story is that having set up camp at Ware—the place names differ—the Danes raided the crops at Hertford, burning what they did not need.

King Alfred decided to put a stop to all this, and either went by boat down the river, or on horseback along the banks (depending on which version is accepted) and, finding a place where the opportunity afforded itself, divided it in three, lowering the waters higher up. The Danes could not sail their ships, and so suffered a crushing defeat.

Another story has it that a barrier was placed across the river, and yet another suggests that the river was tidal, and a barrier across the river near Stratford prevented the tide going up. Most of the legends of the campaign were demolished by Arthur C. Jones, in 1969. The facts were set out in the Anglo-Saxon Chronicle, the only contemporary authority.

It says: "894 . . . In early winter the Danes who were encamped on Mersea rowed their ships up the Thames and up the Lee. That was two years after they came across the sea.

"895. And in the same year the aforesaid army made a fortress by the Lee, 20 miles above London. Then afterwards in the summer a great part of the citizens and also of other people marched till they arrived at the fortress of the Danes, and there they were put to flight and four king's thegns were slain. Then later, in the autumn, the king encamped in the vicinity of the borough while they were reaping their corn, so that the Danes could not deny them that harvest. Then one day the king rode up along the river, and examined where the river could be obstructed, so that they could not bring the ships out. Then they abandoned the ships and went overland till they reached Bridgnorth on the Severn and built that fortress. Then the English rode after the enemy, and the men of London fetched the ships, and broke all which they could not bring away, and brought to London those which were serviceable. And the Danes had placed their women in safety in East Anglia before they left that fortress."

Firm facts are re-established in 911, when the Chronicle states that Edward the Elder, the son of King Alfred, inherited the city of London from his sister, the Queen of Mercia. In November of that same year, he ordered the construction of a burh (fortified place) at Heorutforda (the West-Saxon spelling, as opposed to the Mercian of Bede), north of the River Lee. The following summer Edward marched into Essex to fortify Whitham. The men of Essex submitted to him, and he then built another burh at Hertford on the south bank of the Lee.

Little is known of the site of the northern borough except that it was built between the Rivers Lee, Beane, and Mimram. This suggests that it could have been at Old Cross where stood the Saxon church of St. Mary the Less and a market. The southern borough included St. Nicholas church, sited in the area of the Abbey National Building Society office in Maidenhead Street, and the market place where the Shire Hall now stands. Gordon Davies, Hertford's museum curator, suggests that the centre of the original borough was west of Green Street, now part of Bircherley Green shopping complex.

There is also evidence that the eastern boundary was Ashbourne Ditch. This ditch, bringing water down from the uplands of Brickendon, now takes an abrupt turn from north to east by All Saints churchyard opposite the east end of the church, and then follows a lengthy course to the Lee some distance from the town. But the main ditch may have continued straight on by the west wall of what used to be the old grammar school (and is now a schools' library centre), down the east side of the Dimsdale Arms yard, across Fore Street, down the east side of the Corn Exchange, across Railway Street, through Bircherley (formerly Butchery) Green to the former Dye's Dipping Place on the the Lee where also, at one time, the town's sewer discharged. The ford which connected the twin boroughs was about 50 yards below Mill Bridge. It would be wrong to think of these fortified places as having castles. They were really areas enclosed by palisading and perhaps an earthwork.

A Reeve was set over these Royal burhs and he collected rents from the inhabitants, who were tenants of the King, and the dues, which were paid for the privilege of carrying on a trade under royal protection. Each borough had its Home Guard. All able-bodied men would be organised for garrison-service. Not unnaturally this caused resentment, as it took men from the fields, malting, grinding, and other occupations.

Although the twin boroughs were intended to be a northerly point in a circle of fortified places, there is nothing to suggest that they played any part in the defences when another wave of invaders attacked the country at the beginning of the 11th century, setting up the Danish kingdom of Swein and Canute.

Yet as a fortified town, Hertford provided security for the holding of a market. The Saxon kings, starting at Athelstan (925), followed the practice existing in other boroughs and minted coins at Hertford. The first two Norman kings, William I and II continued the Hertford mint until, during the reign of William II provincial mints were reorganised. Many, including Hertford, were closed down.

King Edgar (957–975) is reputed to have made the town "capital" of the surrounding "shire". It was the usual custom to call the shire by the name of its principal borough.

It was the importance of Hertford in the scheme of defence which probably gave it the edge over St. Albans, even though the Abbey there promoted attention and prosperity.

The Normans brought documentary order with them, and the Domesday Survey shows that Hertford consisted of 10 hides (a hide was 120 acres) of land; there were 146 burgesses (this meant the heads of families, exclusive of women and children); two churches—probably St. Mary the Less and St. Nicholas and the two markets. There were also three mills. The town's chief trade seemed to have been in corn and flour, and London was its chief outlet.

Hertford by then had a motte and bailey defensive structure. This consisted of a large earthen mound—still to be seen near the Castle gates—topped by a strong wooden tower. A moat, fed by the Lee, surrounded the foot of the mound and extended so as to enclose a small yard or bailey in which stood the hall. The castle was like those depicted on the Bayeux tapestry.

The Normans also brought with them a Continental system of local government. At Hertford, instead of the equality of all the townsmen under the King's Reeve, in came a select body of burgesses, governing the borough with privileges and authority over the rest. They elected, from among themselves, a Bailiff to be chief of the "corporation" and to represent the King. He was elected annually, and provided with £1 a year with which he was to buy a robe to mark him out above his fellows. This was a generous allowance, because the sum rendered to the Crown as "fealty-money" in return for the borough's privileges, was only £8. A steward was also elected to preside over the borough court.

As a Royal Borough, Hertford was also liable to "tallage" which was the equivalent of the "aid" paid by baronial tenants-in-chief, to meet the family emergencies of the sovereign. A wedding counted as an emergency, it appears, because the town had to pay £18·50 to meet the expenses of the wedding of Princess Maud, daughter of Henry II, to the Duke of Saxony.

Another bothersome effect of the Norman conquest was that the Saxon village of Ware was placed by William I under the supervision of the Bailiff of Hertford. Not unnaturally this upset the Ware folk. When the bailiff barred Ware bridge with an iron gate, chain, and padlock open hostility broke out.

It was justifiably claimed that traffic was diverted from Ware, and horses and carts had to go through Hertford, and pay toll there. This feud between the two towns continued for centuries and people still live in Hertford who can remember pitched battles between the youths of both towns on the Meads.

On a more religious note, another product of the Conquest was the foundation of Hertford Priory, by Ralph de Limesi, one of William's strongest supporters. It was built on the Lee near the present Priory Street. Richly endowed, it was dedicated to St. Mary. The Priory owned the hide of land on which it was built, and 2½ hides at Pirton, together with the right of presentation of a minister to Pirton Church. Pasture on the Meads, and a mill—Dicker Mill, now a small industrial estate—were added.

The Priory was a cell under the Abbot of St. Albans, who sent six monks to Hertford, with the exclusive duty of praying for the souls of the founder and his family, and holding services for them. In the end de Limesi entered the priory as a monk, and his wife as a sister. An agreement was made with the Abbot that both might be buried in the Priory if, at the time of their deaths, the foundation had gained sufficiently in importance for this to be desirable.

If not they would be buried at St. Albans. De Limesi became Prior, and both he and his wife were buried in the priory cemetery.

Above right: King Alfred the Great. Above left: King Egbert. Below right: King Canute or Cnut.

Below left: A silver penny of Ethelred the Unready made at Hertford by Edwi. On
the obverse is "Aethelraed Rex Anglorx", and on the reverse "Edwi Mo Heort".
991-997.

Above right: Silver penny of Edward the Confessor made by Saemaer at Hertford.
On the obverse is "Eadwarrd Rex", and on the reverse, "Saemaer on Heortf". 1059-1066.

Left: A silver penny of Cnut, made by Leofric at Hertford.
On the obverse is 'Cnut Rex", and on the reverse "Leofric on Heo." 1016-1035. Below right: William the Conqueror.

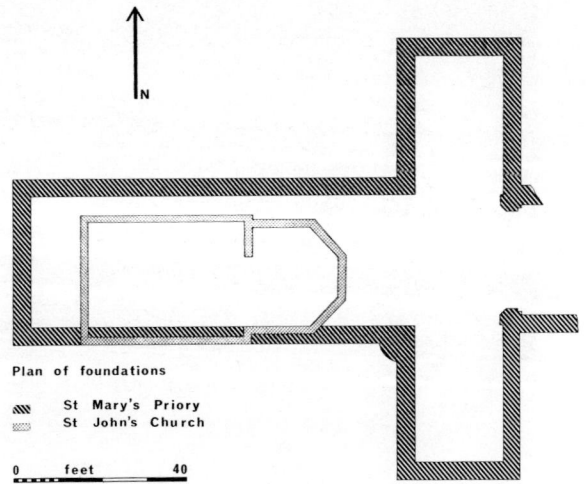

Plan of foundations

▨ St Mary's Priory
▧ St John's Church

0   feet   40

Above: A silver penny of Harold I made by Godman at Hertford. On the obverse is
"Harold Rex", and on the reverse "Godman on Heor". 1038-1040.

Below right: A plan based on the excavations of the foundations, of Hertford Priory.
(Drawn by Gordon Davies.)

Below left: A tile from Hertford's Priory.

Burgū Hertforde p̄ .x. hidis se defend. T.R.E. 7 modo no fact. Ibi mann̄ .c.xl.vi. burgenses in soca regis Eduardi.

Habuit ibi in com Alan .iii. domos. que te modo reddt consuetudine.

Eudo dapifer hb .ii. domos que fuer Algari 7 no reddeb consuetud. 7 tcia domū que tenuit Eudo quā fuit Vlmari non reddt consuetud.

Goisfrid de bech .iii. domos consuetud reddentes.

Hunfrid de Ansleuile ten sub Eudone .ii. domos cū uno horto. harū una accomodata fuit cuidā pfecto regis. 7 altera cū horto fuit cuidā burgensis. 7 in reclamant ipsi burgenses sibi iuste ablatas.

Alios .xviii. burgenses hb roc W. qui fuer Heraldi 7 Leuuini. oms consuetud reddt.

Petrus de ualonges hb .ii. ecclas cū una domo. quas emit de Vluui de haisfelde. reddt oms consuetudines. Ipse Vluui 7 dare 7 uende poterat.

Goisfrid de magneuile hb occupatū qdda que fuit Ingari stalri. 7 vii. domos nullam consuetudine reddider. nisi geldū regis qdo colligebatur consuetud reddt.

Radulf bainard hb .ii. domos. 7 tc 7 modo.

Tund arduin de Scalers hb .xiii. domos. qs habuit ldm. T.R.E. nullā consuetud dabant nisi geldū regis. de qb aduocat harduin regem ad ptectorem. Adhuc unā domū hb harduin de dono regis. que fuit cuidā burgis. reddt ome consuetudine.

Hoc suburbium reddt .xx. lib arsas 7 pensatas. 7 ii. molini reddt .x. lib ad numerū. Eudo pcius uicecomes recep .xv. lib ad numer. reddeb T.R.E. vii. lib 7 x. sol ad numerū

.i. Rex Willelmus.
.ii. Archieps cantuariensis.
.iii. Eps Wintoniensis.
.iiii. Eps Londoniensis.
.v. Eps Baiocensis.
.vi. Eps Lisiacensis.
.vii. Eps Cestrensis.
.viii. Abbas de Ely.
.x. Abb de Westmonast.
.x. Abb de S Albano.
.xi. Abbatissa de Ceriz.
.xii. Canonici de Lundonia.
.xiii. Canonici de Waltham.
.xiii. Comes moritoniensis.
.xv. Comes Alanus.
.xvi. Comes Eustachius.
.xvii. Comes Rogerius.
.xviii. Rotbt de Olgi.
.xix. Rotbt gernon.
.xx. Rotbt de Todeni.
.xxi. Adulf de Todeni.
.xxii. Adulf de limesi.
.xxiii. Adulf bainard.
.xxiiii. Ranulf fr Ilgeri.
.xxv. Hugo de Grentemaisnil.
.xxvi. Hugo de belcamp.

.xviii. Willelmus de o.
.xx. Willelm de odburguile.
.xxi. Walterius flandrensis.
.xxx. Eudo dapifer.
.xxxi. Edward sarebergensis.
.xxvii. Goisfrid de mannenile.
.xxiii. Goisfrid de bech.
.xxiii. Goisbertus de beluaco.
.xxv. Petrus de ualonges.
.xxvi. Vis arduin de Escalers.
.xxx. Edgar.
.xxvii. Magno brito.
.xx. Gislebtus filius salomonis.
.xl. Sugar de Cioches.
.xli. Deruman 7 alii anglici regis.
.xlii. Ricohais uxor Ricardi.
.xliii. Aeliz uxor hugonis.
.xliiii. filia Radulfi tailgebosch.

Terra Regis. In Braughinge hund.
Willelm Rex ten Weruuesdat p̄ viii. hid se defd. Tra ē .xviii. car. In dnio .ii. hide 7 dim. 7 ibi sunt .iii. car. 7 xxiiii. uilli sun focha 7 vi. bord. 7 v. cote hnt .xv. car. Ibi vi. serui. 7 ii. molini de .xx. sol. 7 u .i. car. 7 ii. bob pasta ad pecun uille. Item ad sepe. hoc ō fuit in dnio eccle s marie de ceriz. sed heralt comes abstulit inde ut tota sira testat. 7 apposuit in his maneriosis suis tbz annis ante morte regis Eduardi.

Rex W. ten Meulessene p̄ iiii. hid se defd. Tra ē vii. car. In dnio .ii. hb 7 iiii. 7 dim. 7 ibi sut .iii. car. pbr cū xi. uillis 7 iii. cote hnt .iii. car. 7 adhuc .ii. pot fiere. Ibi .vi. serui. pti .i. car. pasta ad pecun uille. Silua .xxx. porc. Hoc ō iacuit 7 iacet in his Heralt tenuit.

Hertford's entry in Domesday Book.

29

Above: Drawing of the Priory House, a late 16th century building. The eastern part was demolished in 1860, and the remainder in 1906.

Below: An 11th century pottery platter found at the Green Dragon Inn. The inn is on the site of an earlier structure which existed from at least 1621. It is now offices and shops.

Interior and exterior of the Tithe Barn at Hertford Priory. Mediaeval in date, the barn
was demolished in 1900.

Above right: Stephen King of England.

Below right: Henry I.

Left: Speed's map of 1610 shows the castle in detail, (enlarged).

Castle and Kings

The Norman concept of a castle differed greatly from the Saxon. A Saxon fortified area was there to protect the inhabitants of the borough, but the Norman castle was built to overawe the inhabitants and the surrounding districts. In fact it was often used to quell the rebellious people of the borough.

After William II the castle was a Royal retreat, a place of confinement—both for safety and maternity purposes—and a prison. It was handy to London, and a pleasant spot for hunting, hawking, and other country pastimes.

For 300 years the townspeople enjoyed the pomp and pageantry as the court moved into the castle, and probably suffered less than most from the ravages of civil conflict and war.

When the 18 year civil war broke out between Henry I's daughter Matilda, and his nephew Stephen of Blois, it seemed Hertford supported Matilda, because the son of the first governor, Roger de Valoignes, was confirmed as governor for life. His father, Peter de Valoignes, had been appointed the first governor of the castle and its manor by William the Conqueror, and was also sheriff of Essex and Hertfordshire.

While rival barons rampaged up and down the country with armies of foreign mercenaries, building illegal castles, torturing peasants, sacking towns and looting monasteries, there is no record of how this affected Hertford, but in 1153 the rival factions came to terms.

Stephen died within the year, and Henry II enlarged and strengthened the old motte and bailey castle on the Continental pattern, giving it a place in the outer line of defences north of London, with Windsor, Berkhamsted, Bishop's Stortford, and Rayleigh. A large sum of money, in comparative terms, was spent on the work—in the region of £10,000 at modern values.

The fort covered an area of about $7\frac{3}{4}$ acres, protected on the north side by the River Lee. On the other side of the inner enclosure was the double deterrent of a high curtain-wall and moat. The outer enclosure was defended by a second moat which ran along the line of the present Castle Street, Parliament Row, and The Wash. Drawbridges and gatehouses gave entrance to the outer enclosures from points in these streets. Similar defences guarded the entrances to the fortress through the curtain-wall and across the inner moat. The high curtain-wall of flint rubble was about seven feet thick, and still stands today, although patched with brick, stone, and squared flints. The gateway probably became the foundations for the gatehouse which can be seen in the Castle grounds. The inner ward housed the king's residence and the garrison.

When the rebellion of the king's sons came to a head in 1173, the Castle was ready, fully provisioned and occupied by a company of knights and men-at-arms.

While Richard I spent most of his time crusading, or in France fighting Philip Augustus, the government was in the hands of William Longchamps, who was also governor of Hertford

Castle.

Hasty repairs were made, under the supervision of William Fitz Wiger and Hugh Fitz Emme, and in 1191 Richard's younger brother John landed in England backed by a threat of an invasion by Philip of France to help him.

His plans were frustrated, both by the loyalty of William Longchamps, and the early return of Richard, but in 1199, when Richard died, John stepped up to take the throne from his elder brother's son, Arthur. He appointed Richard de Montfitchet, Sheriff of Herts and Essex, as governor of the Castle, but not without active opposition.

Robert Fitz Walter claimed it by right, saying that his wife Gunnora was the daughter of Robert de Valoignes and heiress of his brother Peter. They were sons of Roger and grandsons of the original governor Peter de Valoignes. He produced a charter to prove his right, and then, by force garrisoned the Castle with his vassals.

By superior force John scuttled him out. But having shown that you could not play around with the crown, he appointed Robert Fitz Walter as governor of the castle. He held it for 10 years while baronial feeling against the king mounted. John oppressed the country with heavy taxes, and Fitz Walter became a leader of the baronial opposition.

The difficult governor angered the king by putting a stop to the royal dalliance with his daughter. As a result Fitz Walter had to flee to France in 1211, and his castles at Hertford and Benington were confiscated. Later he returned and took a leading part in the barons' great march against the Crown, which ended with Magna Carta.

Fitz Walter appears to have led the contingent which marched from Bedfordshire and Hertfordshire. The barons won a great victory, and·Fitz Walter was reinstated at the castle. But two months later, when John was attempting to pursuade the Pope that the charter was unlawful, Fitz Walter went to France to offer the Crown to Philip Augustus. Plans were made for the Dauphin to come over, and at the time of John's death in October 1216, he and a French army had already arrived and been enthusiastically received.

It has been suggested that Fitz Walter killed the king by giving him a poisoned poached egg—misguided, if true, because the death of John rallied the barons to his son and successor, Henry III, and they opposed the Dauphin.

This gave rise to the first recorded battle at Hertford Castle, before whose walls the Dauphin with his French army arrived in November. The governor was now Walter de Godarvil, a gallant knight, who withstood the siege for nearly a month before he was compelled to surrender. When the castle fell, de Godarvil surrendered up both castle and town to the Dauphin, with all that implied—looting, raping, and all the horrors of an occupying foreign army.

The town's troubles did not end there, for the Lord of the Manor of Ware took the opportunity to break down the chains and gate on the bridge at Ware, losing Hertford the valuable tolls. These rights were never restored.

If that was not enough, Londoners, who had drawn most of their corn supply from the area, had built themselves a granary lower down the river, and any grain that came from Hertford was collected in London barges instead of those of the Hertford burgesses.

The bad lads of the area were also on the rampage, and the Crown ordered the Sheriff of Hertfordshire to construct a gaol in the borough, in addition to the Castle dungeon. With the Castle in the hands of the Dauphin, Fitz Walter put in a claim for custody, but Louis refused on the grounds that an Englishman who had been a traitor to his own King was not worthy of any office of importance.

Henry III was only nine when he was crowned, and the Dauphin's army was eventually defeated at Lincoln. Soon after he had been crowned, Henry granted the town a fair, to be held for eight days after the Feast of SS Simon and Jude, but it was small compensation for the losses sustained.

But if the people were poor, there was plenty of pageantry and excitement. In 1241, when Peter de Thany was governor of the castle a splendid tournament was held on Hartham. Matthew Paris describes it as being "a bowshot from Hertford", but others place the tournament at Ware—a long bow shot.

These tournaments were opposed by the Church, and the Pope had made several attempts to ban them because they caused a wanton loss of life. They were the big spectaculars of the day, the real life counterparts of today's Cecil B. de Mille extravaganzas, except that the blood and the injuries were real and painful.

The Hertford tournament was held under the auspices of Gilbert Marshal, Earl of Pembroke, before a large crowd of noble spectators. The Earl, it seems, was mounted on a charger to which he was unaccustomed, and it was a lively one. The fanfare rang out calling combatants to the lists, the horse took fright, broke its bridle and bolted.

The helpless Earl was unhorsed, but was unable to kick his mail-clad foot clear of the stirrup. He was dragged along the ground by the startled horse, and received injuries from which he died in Hertford Priory, where his panic-stricken squires had taken him. His heart and entrails were buried in the Priory Church and his body taken to London for interment in the Temple Church, after a quarrel over where he should be buried. Sir Robert Say, one of the Earl's knights, and many others were severely wounded at the same tournament.

King Henry then started suffering family difficulties, which inflicted themselves on Hertford. His mother having married again, he was expected to find favours for his new French half-brothers, one of whom, William de Valences, was made governor of the Castle in 1249. He also obtained the Manors of Essendon and Bayford, and the hand of Joan, heiress of the unfortunate Earl of Pembroke.

De Valance was something of a tearaway, violating nearby houses, and murdering people merely for the fun of it. The story goes that he entertained two Friars from Dunstable on a certain Christmas night. The two brothers had a good meal, but the next morning were found dead in mysterious circumstances. Everyone else in the Castle was in wonderful health.

When Simon de Montfort, who succeeded Fitz Walter as leader of the baronial opposition, fought the King at Lewes, Hertford was on the King's side, de Valences fighting with the Crown. The result was that Hertford missed the chance of being among the founder-members of the House of Commons, put into practice by de Montfort in 1265. But de Valences was again on the King's side at Evesham, where de Montfort was beaten. Back in Hertford, it appears that the 1223 order to build a gaol had not been implemented, and in 1290 de Valences strongly opposed the borough's petition to the Crown for the gaol.

On the death of de Valences in May 1296, the Castle reverted to the Crown, by this time Edward I. He entrusted the manor to a succession of farmers until he gave it to his Queen, Margaret of France, sister of Philip IV, King of France, on their wedding day, September 10th, 1299. But it was not until five years later that he told the people of Hertford about the gift.

An old document amongst the Hertford Corporation papers, dated June 21st, 1304, reads:

"Edward by the Grace of God, King of England, Lord of Ireland, and Duke of Aquitania, to all whome these present letters may come, greeting. Know ye that whereas we have assigned in dowry to Margaret Queen of England, our most dear Consort . . . the Castle and town of Hertford, with its members and all its appurtenances in the county of Hertford . . . To have and to hold to the said Margaret in dowry as long as she shall live, with all the liberties, customs etc., to them belonging, in the same manner as if we ourselves held them . . . We will that the said Margaret shall hold the said Castle etc., as in our letters patent is more fully set forth etc."

In 1298 Hertford sent its first M.P.'s to parliament. The Freemen of the Borough voted in John de Westreete and Simon de Balle, owner of Balls Park. They went to York, because in those days parliament met wherever the King happened to be. Their expenses, paid by the borough, were 4p a day for as long as parliament was in session.

The King visited the Castle a number of times. In 1304 the Sheriff of Herts and Essex was ordered: "Whereas the King proposes to hawk with his goshawks and sparrow-hawks by the rivers in the counties of Essex, Hertford and Middlesex, he orders him to cause all bridges over the river of La Luye (Lee) between the towns of Hertford and Stratford to be well and sufficiently repaired, as Thomas de Wedon, the King's yeoman, whom the King is specially sending to him, shall make known to him on the King's behalf."

In 1309 the Castle was first used for political prisoners, when the Templars from Temple Dinsley, near Hitchin, were housed there. The Templars had ended their useful work in the Holy Land, and had returned rich, and unpopular with the King. The order was suppressed in 1309, and the four Templars were imprisoned in the Castle for six months. Edward II, too, ordered bridges to be cleared in the area so that he could "sport thereon".

The Templars enjoyed some sympathy locally and consequently the new governor of the Castle, Geoffrey de la Lee had a rough time. His weights and measures were smashed, his rent-collectors beaten-up, and his tenants, according to an ancient document, did commit other "orrible and abhomynable dedis." The Castle was now in the hands of Queen Isabella, Edward II's queen, who was described in her early days as the "She-wolf of France, who tearest the bowels of they mangled mate."

In 1330 Isabella fell, and lost the Castle. A year later and back in favour, she returned to Hertford where she remained for most of her life. Edward, meanwhile, either because he had some affection for his mother, or because he wanted to keep an eye on her, visited Hertford frequently, and for quite long periods. Queen Isabella died at the Castle on August 22, 1358, and was buried in the choir of the church of the Grey Friars, Newgate.

Above right: Henry II.

Left: Silver penny of Henry II found in the Angel Yard Barn at Bircherley Green;
made by John at London, 1251-1272.

Below right: Richard I.

Below: Anglo-Gallic casting counter, 14th century, found during the making of the Hertingfordbury bypass.

Above left: King John.
Above centre: Henry III.
Above right: Edward I.

Edward III.

Edward II

39

Letter to the townspeople of Hertford from Edward I telling them he had given the castle to his queen.

Below: Part of the ancient wall of the castle gate house, discovered during alterations.

Royal Prison

In the mid-14th century, the town greeted two royal prisoners-of-war. With Edward III away in France, David Bruce, (David II of Scotland), in support of his country's old ally, moved in through the back door, but his efforts ended in his defeat at Neville's Cross. He was brought to Hertford with his wife, Edward's sister Joan, for a comparatively comfortable exile in his own quarters, until 1357, when he was released under the Treaty of Berwick.

The next royal prisoner was King John of France, captured by Edward's heir, the famous Black Prince, at Poitiers. He spent four months at Hertford, April-July 1359. Both prisoners enjoyed a remarkable degree of freedom, and doubtless did the tradespeople of the town a deal of good. King John was surrounded by colourful and boisterous followers, who boated on the Lee, hunted and hawked on the Meads, and provided their own entertainments in which the townspeople shared.

There then entered John of Gaunt, third son of Edward III. Born at Ghent, at the age of 19 he had married his cousin Blanche, only child of the Duke of Lancaster, and in 1360 the King conferred on him the Castle and Honor of Hertford. The death of his father-in-law made him one of the country's greatest landowners and wealthiest men, but John spent much time at the Castle, which he viewed as his premier home when not in France or Spain, fighting his country's wars.

The Castle was occupied by his three wives and their families, one after the other: Blanche, whose son Henry Bolingbroke later became first Lancastrian King of England Henry IV; Constance; and Catherine, his mistress and governess to his daughters, and who had borne him children before his marriage to her.

But the death of Edward III in 1377, and of the Black Prince in 1376, brought to the throne John's eleven-year-old nephew, Richard II and his first act was to take the Castle away from John of Gaunt—and then give it back to him. But times were difficult and fanned by the oratory of John Ball, and the organising ability of Wat Tyler, in 1381, the peasants revolted. Hertford remained quiet, but St. Albans was in a turmoil because the Abbot was an oppressive landlord. As a result 18 peasants, led by John Grindecobbe, were sent to the dungeons of Hertford Castle pending execution.

Meanwhile Richard II was having a hard time on the throne, and a band of the nobility, calling themselves "The Appellants", eventually protested at his misgovernment. When his first wife Anne, died, he was driven to marry again. It appears that out of spite for his critics, he married eight-year-old Princess Isabella, which meant that there would be no prospect of a direct heir to the throne for many years.

John of Gaunt died soon after his son Henry had been banished by the King for 10 years. This broke the old man up, and on his death King Richard confiscated all the Lancaster estates, including the Castle and Honor of Hertford. But Henry returned and defeated

Richard, and it was at his father's Castle at Hertford that the formal charge was drawn up, accusing Richard II of 33 acts of misbehaviour. Henry was acclaimed king, and in the following year, 1400, Richard was murdered in Pontefract Castle.

Henry IV, on his second marriage in 1402, to Joan of Navarre, granted the Castle to her, but while he was away fighting against King Robert III of Scotland, another royal prisoner appeared at the Castle. He was 12-year-old James, heir to the Scottish throne. A year after his capture he became King James I but he remained at Hertford Castle for 17 years, while moving around with the English court.

When Henry IV died in 1414, the queen retained the Castle by permission of her stepson, Henry V. But in 1418, she was accused of arranging her husband's death by witchcraft. Disgraced, she was deprived of all her possessions. This left the way clear for Henry V to confer the Castle on his new wife, Princess Katherine of France. They spent many happy hours at the Castle until the King's death within 14 months of his marriage.

It was during Henry V's reign that the town successfully petitioned the Crown, asking that it might be exempt from the burden of sending two members to represent it in the House of Commons. It was a question of expense. The trouble was parliament met wherever the Court was, and in the 21 parliaments to which Hertford had sent members between 1298 and 1420, 12 were in London, three at Northampton, two at York, and one each at Carlisle, Lincoln, Nottingham, and Ripon.

Queen Katherine did not stay long at the Castle after Henry's death, because on her marriage to Sir Owen Tudor, her Clerk of the Wardrobe, she automatically lost her royal privileges and estates. Her son, however, retained possession of it.

Henry VI was a popular visitor to the Castle, and one Easter, when he visited the town, he was so touched by the warmth of his reception, that he granted a Charter to the Borough, which confirmed previous privileges, and added some new ones.

This charter of 1441 set out that in order not to interfere with the Thursday and Saturday markets at Hertford, no other markets were to be held within a seven-mile radius on those days, and if they were, the goods exposed for sale were to be forfeited to the Bailiff of Hertford. Consternation in Ware!

Margaret of Anjou, whom Henry married in 1445, was granted the Castle, and also gave privileges to the Borough, which granted the Bailiff and Constable of Hertford permission to hold a horse-fair within the borough boundary. It appears that previously it had been held outside the town, and many rogues had got away without paying the toll collected by the Bailiff on the buying and selling of animals.

By 1455 Henry VI was hopelessly insane and the rival roses of York and Lancaster jockeyed for power. Hertford supported the red rose of Lancaster—and it is that red rose which appears on the Standard of the Honor, granted in 1925. With the House of York in the ascendant, Edward IV granted the Castle to his wife, Elizabeth Woodville, and the line looked safe with two boys and several girls.

Edward died in mysterious circumstances in 1483, and Richard Crookback became Richard III. The two sons of Edward became the Princes in the Tower, where they were murdered. Their mother was deprived of Hertford Castle, which was granted to the Duke of Buckingham, one of the new king's strongest supporters.

But over in France Henry Tudor met a disenchanted Buckingham, who was found to be intriguing with him, and so lost his Castle and his head. Then, Henry Tudor came, conquered and married Elizabeth of York, daughter of Elizabeth Woodville, thus uniting Red and White Roses. He re-granted the Castle to Elizabeth Woodville, and, as a good son-in-law should, restored her to full favour.

Above left: King John of France, a royal prisoner.

Below: Master Revel lived at Bengo when King John was a prisoner at the castle, and this is how Revel's Hall, Bengeo, looked in 1940.

Above right: John of Gaunt, King of Castile and Leon, Duke of Lancaster.

43

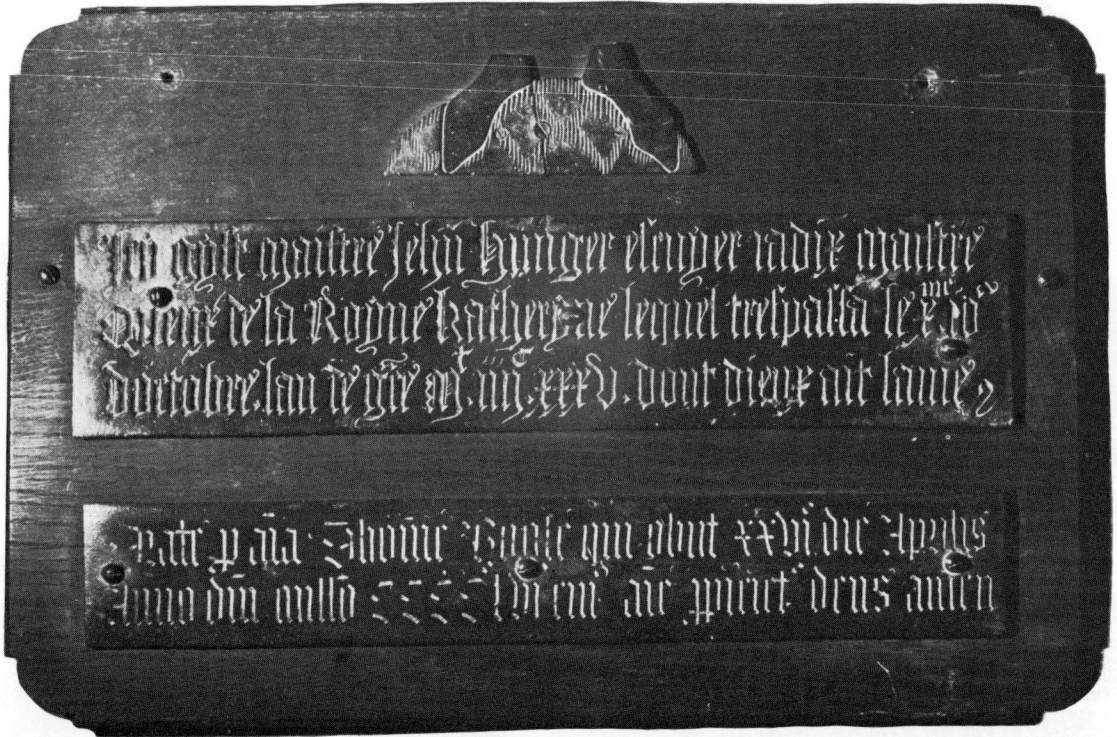

Above left: Richard II.

Above centre: Henry IV

Above right: Henry VI.

Below: Survivor of the fire which burnt down All Saints Church.
Memorial to John Hunger, head chef of Queen Catherine, who died in 1435.

44

Margaret of Anjou with Edward, Prince of Wales, painted in 1801 by Hertford artist, Richard Westall.

Above left: Edward IV.
Above right: Edward V.
Below: Richard III.

Regal Retreat

Elizabeth Woodville did not stay long, for in 1486 all her dower lands were taken away and given to her daughter, Queen Elizabeth. The King kept Easter at the Castle on May 8th, 1489, and was there again on May 25th, 1498.

Henry VII did not visit Hertford often, but his son Henry VIII spent a lot of money on the fabric of the Castle—but with a difference. In the past it had been to improve or repair the fortifications, but now it was to turn it into a civilian palace, with a setting of pleasure-grounds or parks. Of all that building, only the gate house survives, and part of that was built in circa 1465, by Edward IV.

The Castle now became a royal nursery, occupied by Henry's various queens, although Henry did visit the castle with Queen Katherine of Aragon, her daughter Mary, and Sir Thomas More, his friend and chancellor.

The King certainly visited the Castle in June, 1528, and did not enjoy it. Sir J. Russell, writing from Hertford on June 26th, tells Wolsey "The King is much troubled with this disease of sweat."

With the king's marriage to Anne Boleyn, and the birth of Princess Elizabeth, Princess Mary, who had been living at Beaulieu, was moved to Hertford. Spanish Ambassador, Chapuys, in a letter to Charles V wrote: "Nothing new has occurred except that the King has caused the Princess to dislodge from a very fine house to a very inconvenient one." Her stay was short and she was moved to Hatfield, to join her sister.

In December, two years later, the two Princesses were staying at the castle. At the time Thomas Lord Cromwell, Privy Seal, was arranging a marriage for Mary with the German Protestant Prince Duke Philip of Bavaria. It was Lord Cromwell who told Princess Mary of the proposed marriage when he visited the castle.

Anne Boleyn went, and Jane Seymour had, in 1537 given birth to a son Edward. On November 8th, 1545 he was at Hunsdon, but on January 11th, 1546, he joined his sisters at the castle.

By this time, in common with many other towns, Hertford had lost its Priory, in the Dissolution in 1536 of the Lesser Monasteries. A year afterwards, the King conferred the property on one of his Privy Councillors, Anthony Denny, who was later knighted.

Meanwhile Princess Elizabeth, now 12, was preparing a book to be presented to the Queen. She translated and copied out in Latin, French, and Italian, prayers and meditations selected by the Queen from various English writers. The volume is among the Royal manuscripts at the British Museum. On it are the initials R.K.P. and the Sacred Monogram worked in blue silk and silver thread by Elizabeth. It is dated: Hertford, December 20th, 1545.

Prince Edward, too, wrote many letters from the Castle, and he was there when Henry

VIII died. Once he was crowned Edward VI, at the age of nine, he never visited Hertford again, but granted the Castle to his sister, Mary. Meanwhile Elizabeth was at Hatfield.

His Protestant reforms in religion, which caused such difficulties in other parts of the country, found the Hertford clergy in the same category as the musical Vicar of Bray, who sang: "Whatsoever King may reign, I'll still be the Vicar of Bray sir."

The Vicar of All Saints, John Matreyvers remained in office from 1537 to 1557, and at St Andrew's, Rector John Lorynge, who died in 1550, must have put the changes into effect.

Mary Tudor succeeded her brother in 1553, and with the Roman Catholic restoration, Hertford's castle gaol was used as a prison for local Protestants; both parish priests survived the change.

Mary granted the town another Charter on February 17th, 1554, in which customs already established and granted in previous charters, were, for the first time collected under the Royal Seal. Queen Elizabeth subsequently granted a further Charter to the Borough in 1588, but with several alterations and additions. She often came to Hertford, and in 1561 spent £1,975/2/3½ on a 16-day visit.

It is believed that during the plague in London, Law Courts and Parliament were moved to Hertford Castle; certainly high officials of the Crown and Court moved to Hertford, great care being taken to ensure they had diets to which they were accustomed. The Star Chamber, one of the royal prerogative courts, sat at the Castle, as did the Privy Council. The Castle was chosen as a safe place to house Mary, Queen of Scots, though she was eventually confined at Tutbury.

The plague did not confine itself to London, but hit Hertford with great severity in the years 1573, 1576, 1596 and 1597. St Andrew's suffered particularly badly, and in March, 1596, burials mounted to 13, instead of the usual one or two a month, and in the following July the five children of William Manisty, a prominent burgess, later elected Bailiff of the Borough, died within a fortnight of one another.

With the return to Protestantism and the 39 Articles, the clergy, such as vicar of All Saints', Rev. Thomas Noble, (appointed in 1576), found it difficult to adapt to the rubric which called for the preaching of a sermon. He was, we are told "no preacher", and he tried to get others to do the job.

Nonconformity had scarcely begun, but in the last year of Elizabeth's reign a child was born and baptised at All Saints —Samuel Stone, of whom we shall hear more later.

The death of Elizabeth (1603) brought the end of the pomp and glory of the Castle, which became a private house. Tradition gives it a secret passage to Queen's Hill (Queen's Road) but no trace has been found. There is also a spring in a Queen's Hill garden which was formerly known as the Queen's Cup and Saucer. It was surrounded by a double row of stones and was also sometimes called the Queen's Bath.

James I forsook the Castle and left Hatfield House in favour of Theobalds Palace, but in 1621 John Norden, a deputy to the Surveyor-General of Prince Charles, made a survey of Hertford.

He wrote: "The Castle of Hertforde with the appurtenances is parcell of the deamesnes of the said Mannor of Hartford, and is in lease unto Thomas Mewtys Esq.; at the yearely rent of tenne shilling but for what terme yet to come they know not, and that there are lying betweene the said Burrow and a certain Meade called Wrange Mead seven ozier beeds ioyninge to the riuer of lee conteyninge about one acre and a halfe, and that the Channell and Streme of the said riuer of Lee and the fashinge and Rioltie thereof beinge at the East End of Hertingefordeberry parke and extindinge to a certain ditche called blacke ditche next Ware and the Meads called Castle Meades lyinge near vnto the said Harting-fordeberry parke conteyninge about xxiiii Acres are now in the hands of Sir William Harrinton Knight for what terme of yeares of what yearely rent the said Jurors knowe not."

In September 1628, Prince Charles, now King Charles I granted the Castle to William Cecil, second Earl of Salisbury. It has remained in the ownership of the Salisbury family until the present day.

Over the last three hundred years the Castle has had many distinguished tenants, including the Cowper family, but the Marquess, continuing a practice started in 1911, now leases it to the town.

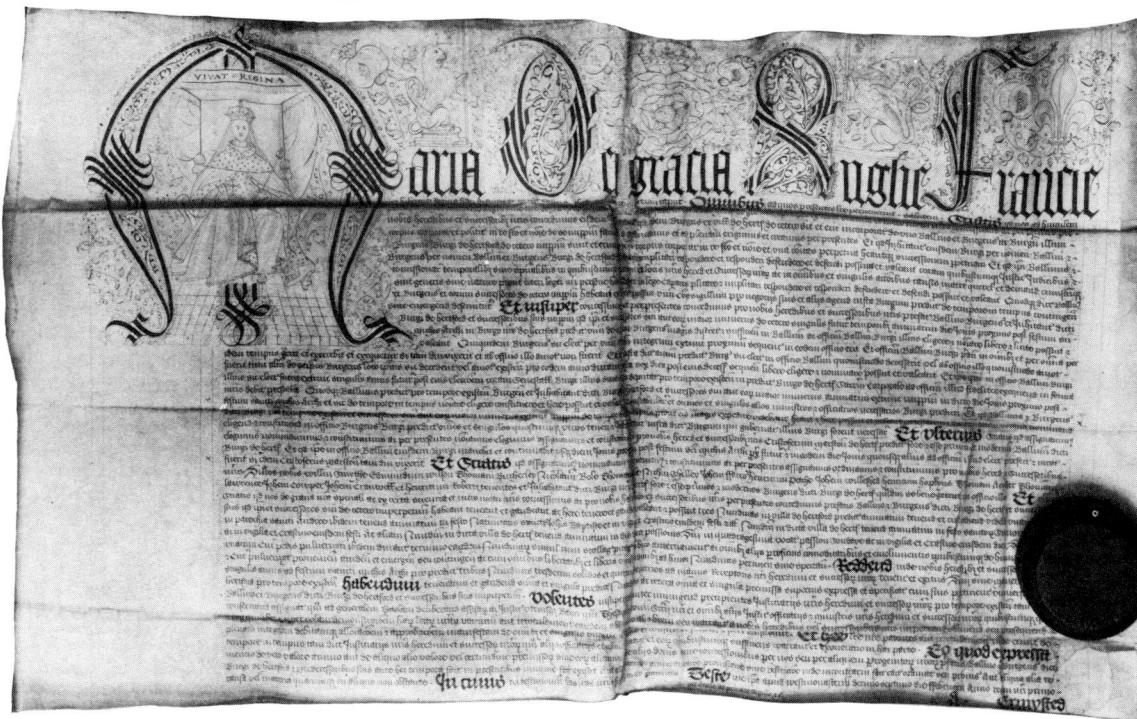

Above left: Henry VII. Above centre left: Henry VIII.

Above centre right: King Edward VI.

Above right: Queen Mary I.

Below: The charter given to the town by Queen Mary.

49

Above: The grant of a market to the town by Queen Mary.

Below: Portrait by an unknown artist of Princess Elizabeth at the age of 12.

estimabit, quam aliud vllum
ornametũ, et sentiet diuinũ hoc
opus, quod est pluris estimãdum.
quia à serenyssima regina cõiuge
tua, colligebatur, paulo in maiori
precio habendũ esse, quia abs filia
tua conuertebatur. Ille rex regum.
in cuius manu corda regũ sũt, ita
gubernet animũ tuum, et vitã tue-
atur, vt in vera pietate, ac religione
diu sub maiestatis tuę imperio diu
viuamus   Harfordiæ 20
die decembris
1545

ignorationem, ętatem, breue tẽ-
pus studij, et voluntatem, veniã
mertur. et si mediocre sit, etiã
si nullam laudem mereatur, ta-
men si bene accipiatur, me vehe-
menter excitabit vt quantum
annis cresco, tantum etiam sci-
entia, et dei timore crescam, itaq̃
fiet vt illum religiosius colam, et
maiestatem tuam officiosius ob-
seruem. Quamobrem nõ dubito,
quin paterna tua bonitas, et re-
gia prudentia, hunc internum
animi mei laborem nõ minoris

Two pages of the book written by Princess Elizabeth, aged 12, when she was at Hertford Castle, in her own handwriting; the date "Harfordia 20 die decembris 1545" is at the bottom of the second page.

Above: Queen Elizabeth I.
Below left: King James I.
Below right: King Charles I.

52

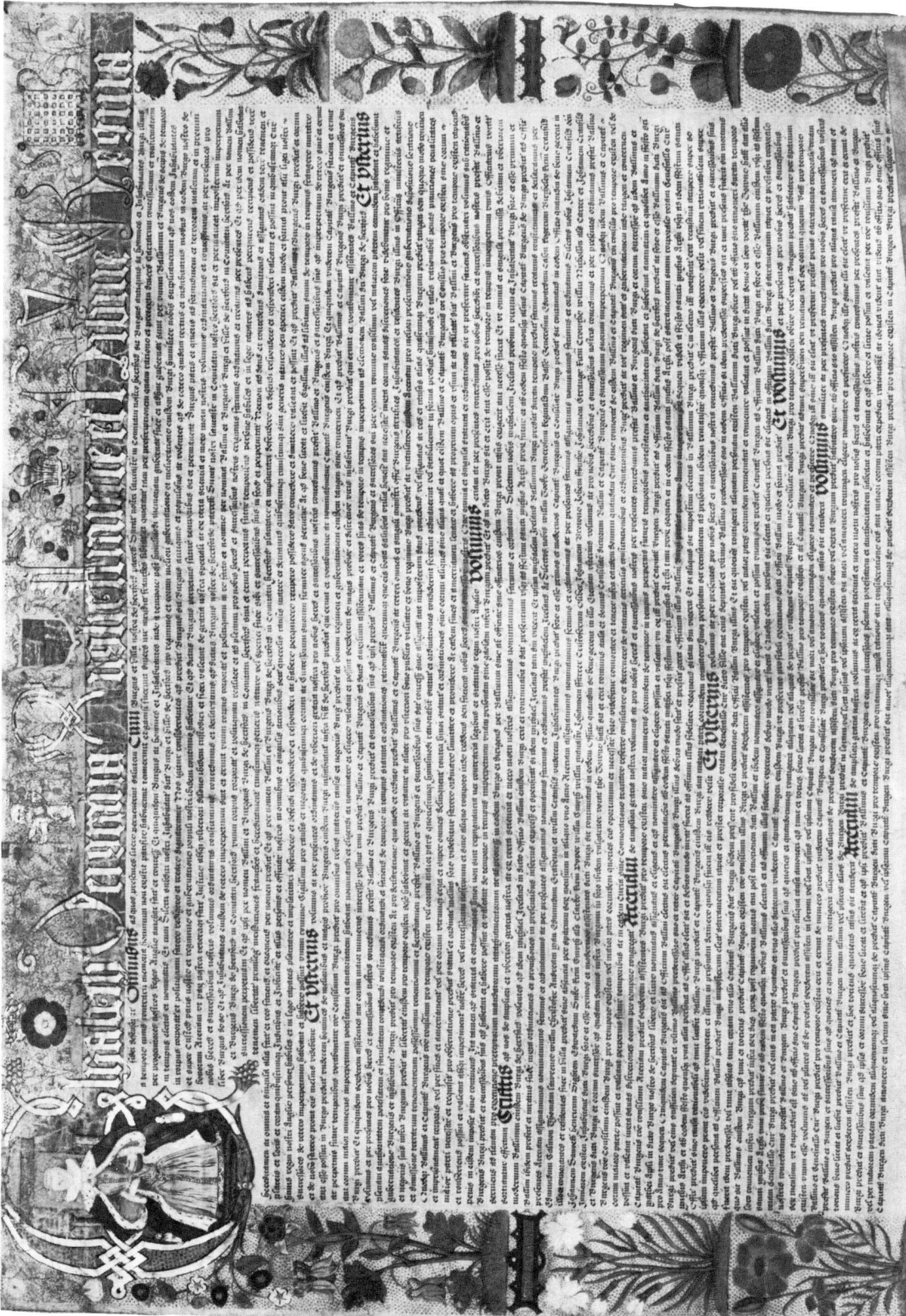

The charter of Queen Elizabeth I.

Above left: Detail of All Saints or All Hallowes, from Speed's map.

Above right: Remains of St Mary the Less, near the public library.

Below: St Leonard's, Bengeo, as it is today.

The Church

From the 673 Synod Hertford kept in step with the established church for many centuries, and once, as well as the Priory, had five churches within its boundaries.

Domesday Survey includes two churches; one in each borough. St Mary's was near the present library and St. Nicholas' in what is now Maidenhead Street, behind the Abbey National Building Society office.

Remains of these two churches are scant, but when the foundations for the library were being dug in 1887 fragments of stonework were discovered. One piece has been set up outside the library, but the altar stone is now merged into the Communion table in the Blessed Sacrament Chapel of St Andrew's Church. The font of St Nicholas' church was all that remained. For some years it was in private hands, but it is in use in the little church at Tonwell, just outside the town's boundary.

The last Rector of St. Mary's was inducted in 1503, and the church pulled down in 1514. The last Rector of St Nicholas' was presented in 1424 and the church demolished in 1675. The parishes were probably united with St Andrew's in about 1707.

At the time of Domesday, the priest, whose stipend was similar to that of a skilled artisan, was granted a double holding of land, was the village schoolmaster—the school was held in the church porch—and sometimes looked after the village bull and arranged its stud appointments.

The Priory Church served the parish of St John and had a double dedication. The choir and transepts were reserved for the monks and dedicated to St Mary (known sometimes as The Great); the nave was the parochial church and dedicated to St John.

When Hertford Priory was dissolved, the nomination to the living was given to Sir Anthony Denny. After some rapid changes, it came into the hands of Thomas Willis, who found the church almost in ruins. In 1629 he rebuilt it on a smaller scale inside the old nave, dedicating it to St John.

In 1637, however, he sold the manor in which it lay, together with the advowson, to Sir John Harrison of Balls Park, and the parish was then united with that of All Saints.

The church was eventually pulled down later in the 17th century by order of the Bishop of Lincoln, in whose diocese the town lay. Not a stone or relic of the old church remains.

The oldest building in the town is St Leonard's Church in Bengeo, a village now within the town boundary. The church stands on a spur of land which overlooks the junction of the rivers Rib and Lee, and was built around 1120, but an earlier one, probably of wood, may have been destroyed by the Danes.

In the 12th century the de Tany family held that part of Bengeo, and in 1156 the Chronicle of Bermondsey Priory registers that Reginald de Tany gave the church to the Priory.

It remained their property, being served by a vicar, until the dissolution of the monasteries, when the patronage fell to the crown. It passed to the Fanshawe family of Ware Park in 1623, and then to the Byde family. In 1846 the Abel Smith family of Woodhall Park purchased the rectorial tithes, and in 1848 turned the living into a rectory.

But in 1855, Holy Trinity was opened, and St Leonard's fell out of use for a time. Now, however, services are held there in the summer on alternate Sunday evenings.

In the entrance is the ancient south doorway of the Norman church. On the left jamb of the doorway are the remnants of a mass dial—a simple form of sundial. It marked the hours of the church services.

The remains of an Anchorite's Cell are behind the panelling against the north wall of the chancel. In this lived an anchorite or hermit, a member of a community of Trinitarian friars who had a small house on the outskirts of Hertford.

When King John of France was a prisoner in Hertford Castle, he visited the church and heard Mass said by a brother of the Trinity on the Wednesday in Holy Week and on Easter Tuesday. While there his hounds worried and killed a sow belonging to Master Revel and he had to pay compensation of 10s. Revel's Hall still stands next to the churchyard.

All Saints and St Andrew's, the two churches in the centre of the town, are the living survivors of ancient parishes. The parish of All Saints' was assigned by Peter de Valoignes' son to the canons of Waltham Abbey, "for the health of" himself and his wife. This would be Roger, who took over the governorship of the Castle in 1141.

The old church of All Saints was burnt down in December, 1891. It was probably an early 15th century rebuilding of an earlier church. It led the way by having the first and only peal of eight bells in the county until 1729, and it shared with St Michael's of Bishop's Stortford, the distinction of being the first in the county to have an organ.

The church also boasted the first known woman organist in the country, Dionisia Battell, a spinster, who in her will of November 17th 1730 gave "all her messuage or tenement, known by the name of the Blue Anchor, situate in the said town of Hertford, for a perpetual encouragement to the organists successively of All Saints' Church in Hertford for ever." It was one of several such endowments.

Another church record was Charles Bridgeman's fame as organist from 1792 to 1873. He started when he was 13, and carried on until he was 94. In the present century W. J. Comley continued this tradition as organist for 50 years.

Because of burglars, the church plate was kept at the vicarage, and this was unaffected by the 1891 fire; of the old church only two tablets remain—both now combined. One is in memory of "John Hunger, master cook to Queen Katherine", wife of Henry V, who died in 1435.

For just over three years, services were held in the Corn Exchange, and the foundation stone of the new building was laid by the Countess Cowper on March 25th 1893. It was dedicated by the Bishop of St Albans on February 20th 1895. Ten years of steady effort were needed before the second stage of the building, the tower, could be completed. Called the Victoria Tower, as a thanksgiving for the reign of Queen Victoria, it was opened by the Bishop on All Saints' Eve, 1905. Two years later the peal of 10 bells was added.

The organ was built in 1898 by "Father" Willis, he built the organ in St Paul's Cathedral —but it was not finished until 1973.

St Andrew is of royal foundation, and the patronage of the living has (with a break of about 40 years at the end of the 14th century) always been vested in the crown. The original church was of Saxon foundation, but it was almost entirely rebuilt in the latter half of the

15th century. By the middle of the 19th century the old church had become "cold, damp and depressing" and efforts were made to raise enough money to rebuild it. The foundation stone of the present church was laid by the Earl Cowper on June 4th, 1869, and the church was consecrated by the Bishop of Rochester (The St Albans Diocese was not formed until 1877) on March 24th 1870.

The old tower remained, but did not suit the new building, so in 1874 Earl Cowper, supported by Mr Robert Smith of Goldings, offered to build a new tower and spire. This was dedicated on February 22nd 1875. The north doorway of the church incorporates the old church doorway.

In the middle aisle of the original building was a gravestone which read "Here lies Richard Pynere, former butler with the Queen of England 1419" together with a representation of a flagon and cup. The tomb had been removed from St Nicholas Church.

Holy Trinity church at Bengeo was built by public subscription, with the support of Abel Smith, and opened for worship in June 1855.

Another church, Christ Church, was built by Abel Smith and opened on June 30th, 1869, but this was pulled down just before it reached its centenary. The donor also built a school to the north of it, which was also used as a church hall. This is now a little theatre, owned by the Company of Players.

The oldest religious house in continuous use in the town is the Quaker Meeting House. This is also the world's oldest surviving Quaker Meeting House to be built as such (1669). Quakers had existed in the town earlier than that: it was a Yorkshire man, James Nayler who brought the faith to Hertford, and his first convert was probably Henry Sweeting, in whose house meetings were held in about 1655. Henry Sweeting ran a butcher's shop in Maidenhead Street—a shop which remained much the same until 1973, when it was demolished.

Many of the Hertford Quakers, including Henry, were flung into gaol during the religious intolerance of the period, mostly for refusing to attend their parish church or refusing to take the oath of allegiance. Some were ordered to be transported, but ship's Captain Thomas May invented a non-existent law for refusing to take them.

Surprisingly enough it was when many of the influential members were in gaol that it was decided to build the meeting house. It possesses a George Fox chair, but it is not known if it was given by the great man himself. He is thought to have made three visits to Hertford.

Nonconformists in the town suffered like the Quakers. They were usually lumped under the one heading as Independents (later Congregationalists, and now United Reformed Church), but they did not have a fixed meeting house, and shared a minister with one at Hitchin.

The first Congregational Church in Hertford was built on a site just to the east of South Street, opposite what is now "The Lord Haig" public house. The site is within the boundary wall of Christ's Hospital, which bought it from the Congregation in 1782. This meeting house was built about 1673. In the 18th century the Congregational Church grew, and houses in Castle Street and St Andrew Street were subsidiary chapels.

Much of the progress was due to John Guyse, a famous dissenting clergyman, and a native of Hertford. At the age of 19 he was assistant to Mr Haworth at the Congregational Church, and was eventually asked to succeed him in 1705. His books on "The Divinity and Person of Christ" and "The Divinity of the Holy Spirit" gained wide interest, not only from dissenters, but also in the Established church. The present church in Cowbridge was built in 1862. John

Wesley visited the town in 1778 and said "I preached to 50 or 60 dull creatures at poor desolate Hertford". But some of this early Methodism remained in various forms, and they built their first chapel in Railway Street (then Back Street) in 1818, and a second in Market Street in 1840. They then built a church in Ware Road in 1867. This has now been rebuilt into a modern structure with linking meeting rooms and a hall.

The Universal British Directory of Trade, Commerce and Manufacture", Hertford section was issued in 1794, and listed two dissenting chapels, as well as the Quaker Meeting House. One of these was the Congregational Chapel, and the other the Ebenezer Strict Baptist Chapel, which was at the junction of North Road and Hertingfordbury Road. The foundation stone bore the date 1773. Since the building of the Hertford Relief Road it was pulled down, and a new chapel built on a site on the opposite side of North Road. The site was formerly occupied by the Cold Bath public house. As the Baptists believe in total immersion as a form of baptism, the site is not inappropriate. The present Baptist Church, at the junction of Cowbridge and Port Hill, was built in 1906.

It was not until the middle of the 19th century that Roman Catholicism came to be re-organised in Hertford, and the present church dedicated to the Immaculate Conception and St Joseph, was built in 1861. Appropriately it is on land which once belonged to the Priory.

There are also in the town several smaller churches. One in Nelson Street houses the Plymouth Brethren. The Salvation Army Citadel was in the bus station, and was formerly the ragged school built by the Quaker draper, William Pollard in 1859. The Citadel is now in Baker Street.

In Port Vale, opposite the school there was a Calvinist Independent Chapel built for a break away congregation from St. Andrew's who followed the rector, the Rev. Bernard Gilpin, when he resigned the living in 1835. The Gospel Hall in Hartham Lane occupies a room of the otherwise demolished Cowbridge House.

Detail of the wallpainting at St Leonard's showing the deposition from the cross. The painting is 13th century.

The present day chancel and arch at St Leonard's.

Above: Interior of the old All Saints before 1886. The east window was altered that year.

Below: All Saints after the fire in 1891.

Above: Workmen pose with the foundation stone of the present All Saints.

Below: All Saints viewed from Gascoyne Way (The Relief Road).

61

Above left: Charles Bridgeman, organist at All Saints for 81 years—a world record.

Above right: John Guyse, an inspiration to the Congregational Church in Hertford.

Below: Interior of All Saints.

A print of All Saints Church made in 1799. Until 1987 this was thought to be St Andrew's Church.

Left: St Andrew's Church today.

Right: The Salvation Army Citadel when it was housed in the former Ragged School.

Above: Hertford's Friends Meeting House, the oldest in the world built for the purpose and still in regular use. Joan Kendall is wearing a Quaker Costume of about 1810.

Below: Garden front of Cowbridge House in Hartham Lane. The property was sold in 1859 for the construction of the railway and most of the house demolished. The drawing room wing on the left has survived. It is now the Gospel Hall and an adjoining house.

Right: The second Marquess of Salisbury.

Left: The Castle from across the River Lee.

Great Houses

Although the Castle was granted to William Cecil, second Earl of Salisbury, he in turn leased it at £10 a year to Sir William Harrington, a Member of Parliament for the Borough in the first year of Charles I, who spent large sums in improving the Castle.

After him came the Cowper family in the person of Sir William Cowper, and he left it to his fourth son Spencer Cowper. He in turn passed the lease to Edward Cox of Cheshunt. Spencer Cowper died in 1676, and at an unrecorded date, Cox assigned the lease to Sir William Cowper, Spencer's nephew.

The Cowper family kept the lease until the early 1700s, and during that century it was occupied by the first Marquis of Downshire. His splendid parties revived memories of the early greatness of the Castle. He also made a number of alterations, including blowing up part of the old curtain wall of the Castle with gunpowder.

But in 1806 the Castle became, as many other great houses, a college—acquired by the East India Company. True, it was only temporary accommodation because the company had bought a nearby estate—Haileybury—with a view to building the college there, but it remained at the Castle until 1809, when the Haileybury buildings were ready for occupation.

For another nine years the Castle was used as a prep school for the college under the headship of Dr Luscombe, who later became a Bishop of the Scottish Episcopal Church, and then reverted to a private house, the residents including Philip Longmore, for 37 years town clerk of the borough, and Alexander Peter McMullen.

The home with the most colourful history is probably Brickendonbury, which may date back to Roman times. In 1893, 430 Roman coins were dug up from the moat—remnants of which still exist. The first recorded occupant of the site was a Saxon, Bricha, who may have held the estate as a steward for the king, and the name is derived from that period.

In the XIth century the land was certainly in the possession of the Saxon Kings, as Edward the Confessor gave it to the Canons of Waltham, and their tenancy is to be found in the Domesday Book. It remained the property of a religious house until Henry VIII dissolved the monasteries, when it returned to the crown. For about 100 years it belonged mainly to Suffolk families. Two Lord Mayors of London lived there in 1598 and 1698. Part of the present mansion, the north front, was built in about 1700. Before that it is believed that three different houses stood on the site.

Additions to the house were later made by the Morgan family who owned the estate from the middle of the 18th to the middle of the 19th century. They planted the fine avenue of trees connecting the estate with Hertford, now known as Morgan's Walk. In 1893 a large part was sold to George Pearson for £30,000, and on his death in 1902, Brickendonbury passed to his son, Sir Edward Pearson, and in 1925 to his wife.

A preparatory school numbered among the occupants between wars, but at the outbreak of the Second World War it took on an important role. The house and grounds became the headquarters of the Special Operations Executive, European Theatre of War.

Many important sabotage and espionage operations were planned and carried out from Brickendonbury and nearby residents tell of German planes, tanks, and other equipment being blown up in the grounds, as saboteurs were taught their job.

The blowing up of the Paris radio station was planned and carried out from Brickendonbury, and the team concerned was back "home" two days later. Odette Churchill (later Hallowes) was trained there.

After the war the estate returned to peaceful purposes, as the local headquarters of the National Agricultural Advisory Service, but in the late 1960s it was unoccupied. In 1971 it was purchased by the Malaysian Rubber Producers' Research Association, and is now owned by the Malaysian Government.

Bayfordbury was mainly built in 1760 by Sir William Baker, who was prominent in raising government loans during the Seven Years War. When he was offered a baronetcy by a grateful nation, he replied "I would prefer a knighthood, for that confines the folly to myself and entails no ridicule on my descendants." In the grounds is a fine group of cedars which were planted in 1765.

Until about 25 years ago the house contained the original portraits of the Kit Cat Club, founded in 1700 by Jacob Tonson. The members decided that their portraits should be painted and presented to Tonson, but the room he built for them was too low, and the painter, Sir Godfrey Kneller, himself a member, limited the size of the pictures to 36ins high by 28ins wide, and the figures, which are life-sized, are only painted down to the waist. They are now in the National Portrait Gallery. The house remained in the Baker family until 1939, and it then became the home of the John Innes Horticultural Institute. The institute moved to Norwich in the early 1960s, and the mansion was part of Hatfield Polytechnic, but has now reverted to housing accommodation.

Another house which contained a wonderful art collection was Panshanger, which was demolished in 1954. It was built by Atkinson in about 1801, on the site of an earlier house. The grounds were landscaped by Repton, the "Red Book" for which is in County Record Office. The house encased a small Elizabethen structure.

The mansion was the seat of the Cowper family, who had earlier lived at Cole Green. After the death of the seventh Earl in 1905, the estates passed to his niece, the noted Edwardian hostess, Lady Desborough, who died there in 1952. In the middle of the 19th century, the art collection amounted to 200 old masters. Legend has it that the German idea of having a Christmas tree was introduced at a party at Panshanger, thus starting the English nobility on a new fashion which is now part of our own Christmas pageantry. The Panshanger Oak, described in 1798 as "probably the finest and most stately oak now growing in the south-east of England" was made the subject of a Tree Preservation Order in 1953.

Goldings, which was the seat of Robert Smith, lies off the main road to Stevenage, and is also owned by the County Council.

The present building was built in about 1877, but it took the place of an earlier, but not long built mansion which was pulled down, it being "somewhat damp, and exposed to the mists arising from the river."

It was Robert Smith, who in 1869 diverted the road to give better access from Hertford to Watton-at-Stone and Bramfield. Included in the cost were five bridges. In 1922 Dr

Barnado's Homes took over the house when it became the William Baker Technical School. The school's printing section is now housed in Mead Lane.

Ware Park is in reality nearer to Bengeo. But it was not until the manor passed into the hands of the Fanshawe family in 1575 that they built the first mansion at Ware Park. It was from these gardens that peaches and grapes were supplied to James I twice a week.

The estate was sold to Sir Thomas Byde, Recorder of London in 1669, and he rebuilt the mansion. It remained in the Byde family until 1829. The house was burnt down in 1911, but rebuilt by the then owner, Mr. W. F. Parker. It later became a chest hospital, and remained so until 1973 when the patients were moved to East Herts Hospital in Hertford. The estate was owned by the Area Health Authority, but the mansion is now used for flats.

Balls Park, now owned by the county council, and used as an annexe of Hatfield Polytechnic probably gave its name to Simon de Balle, one of the burgesses who served the Borough of Hertford. He was one of Hertford's first M.P.'s.

Just before the Norman Conquest the estate may have belonged to King Harold, but Domesday Book listed it as being part of the Manor of Amwell. It was given to the founder of Hertford Priory in about 1080.

When the Priory was dissolved, the estate was confiscated by the Crown, and with the Priory, became the property of Sir Anthony Denny, Gentleman of the Privy Chamber and Groom of the Stool.

The estate changed hands in 1587, in 1590 and again in 1617 when Richard Willis became owner. His son, Sir Thomas Willis was later M.P. for Cambridge, and a violent Royalist. Yet he quarrelled with Charles I, and with the government of Charles II.

John Harrison, a native of Lancaster, and M.P. for that borough, bought the land in 1637, and built the first house. But the household was run, on the death of his wife, by his 15-year-old daughter, Ann, who married Sir Richard Fanshawe of Ware Park. Her father was a Customs farmer, a man who collected Customs revenues for the Crown and speculated with both the receipts and the anticipated collection of future years—a normal practice, but a dangerous one. In the Civil War his estate was taken off him, and only restored after his second wife had pleaded to Parliament that they were destitute.

His grandson Edward, who succeeded in 1725, pursued a distinguished career with the East India Company, and returned to be M.P. for Hertford, as well as improving the house and estate at Balls Park. His younger brother George succeeded him in 1732, and also became M.P. for Hertford.

George was succeeded by Ethelreda Harrison, his niece, and she made a brilliant marriage to Charles Townshend, son and heir of the second Viscount "Turnip" Townshend. Ethelreda (or Audrey as she preferred to be called) was as much an eccentric as her husband. She was a celebrated wit, and estrangement from her husband took place about 1738, after which he made an alliance with one of his housemaids and tried to leave his fortune to her. His wife too had many flirtations, perhaps the most amazing with Lord Kilmarnock, one of the Jacobite lords who was tried and executed for treason after the '45 Rebellion.

Her second son Charles was a brilliant orator and became Chancellor of the Exchequer in 1766. His elder brother George joined the Army and became a Brigadier-General under Wolfe in Quebec and received Montcalm's surrender on the Heights of Abraham as Wolfe lay dead. He was Lord Lieutenant of Ireland in 1767, by which time he was the fourth Viscount. He ended his career as a Field-Marshall.

It was the fifth Marquess, John Villiers Townshend, who lost the family fortunes. He was a philanthropist, known to the London poor as "the good Marquess." The fortune all but went on what his obituary called "unsuccessful schemes for what he hoped might be the improvement of the condition of his less fortunate brethren."

By the 1880s Balls Park was leased to Sir George Faudel-Phillips. On the death of the Marquess in 1889, he bought the estate. Sir George was the second Jewish Lord Mayor of London, his father being the first. He had a distinguished career in the City and entertained lavishly.

His son Sir Benjamin succeeded to the title in 1922, but died five years later, when his brother Sir Lionel succeeded. Sir Lionel twice served the town as Mayor in 1928-29 and 1929-30 without having sat as a councillor.

To mark his years of office he presented to the town a painting by one of Hertford's distinguished residents, Richard Westall. The canvas, "Harvest Storm" hangs in the Shire Hall.

Royal visitors continued to enjoy their stays at Balls Park, one of the most frequent being the present Queen Elizabeth the Queen Mother, a popular visitor to the town.

Sir Lionel gave the town its cricket pitch, and often he would walk straight across the field in mid-over. Play would stop immediately, tea would be brought out for him and, after a suitable pause, the game would go on. He died in 1941, and for four years the house was used for handicapped children evacuated by London County Council, and was then bought by the county council.

The Castle from a print by S. Hooper, published on April 29, 1784.

70

Above: Brickendonbury.

Below: Downstairs at Brickendonbury: the staff pictured in about 1908.

Above: Bayfordbury.

Below: Panshanger now completely demolished.

Below: The library at Panshanger.

Above: The picture gallery at Panshanger with its priceless collection.

Above left: The seventh Earl Cowper, 1834-1905.

Above right: The old house at Goldings demolished in 1868.

Below left: Balls Park.

Below right: Sir John Harrison.

74

Above: Ware Park in about 1910.

Below left: The fourth Marquess Townshend (1795-1863).

Below right: Sir George Faudel Phillips.

Above left: The market cross in 1610 somewhere near the Bell Inn (now the Salisbury). It was probably called the Bell because the market bell hung there.

Below: Sele Roller Mills in North Road, on the site of Tate's Paper Mill.

Above right: Now no longer standing; Ilotts Mill – notice on it once said: "A Mill has stood on this site for 1000 years". Castle Hall is on the site.

Markets and Mills

The products of the field were the main source of income for Hertford in the dim and distant past, but it was the Royal Palace of Hertford—the Castle—which ensured that market.

During the Middle Ages the Saxon market continued in spite of the decline in Hertford's prosperity due to the opening of the bridge at Ware in the 13th century. One of the many commodities sold at the market was wool, and Hertford was noted for its woollen trade even in the 18th century.

The sheep market was held behind the Ram Inn in Fore Street; Dye's Dipping Place, already mentioned, was where the sheep were dipped, and there was an old Woolpack public house, demolished, but rebuilt on the banks of the Lee.

But it was the Kings and Queens of England that frequented the Castle who helped preserve the market through the granting of charters, and their very presence brought prosperity.

When the Castle ceased to be a Royal Palace, Hertford might not have survived as a market town, but in reality this was only the beginning of a major period of prosperity.

The revolution in agricultural methods began in the county towards the end of the 16th century. Then came the use of turnips in the four-course system of crop rotation, introduced by the Townshends of Balls Park into Norfolk.

By the 18th century Hertfordshire was the main corn producing county in England, and by 1831 it was said of Hertford's market: "The business transacted in grain is scarcely equalled in any other provincial market." The growth of London was the magnet for these agricultural products.

In addition trade in barley at Hertford and the production of malt at Ware was tremendous. This was due to the 18th century view that "beer was best".

The corn factors, maltsters, malt-factors, brewers, bankers, insurance companies, barge owners and carters were all closely linked. For instance, the Adams family, barge owners at Ware, and bankers, brewers and maltsters at Hertford, had links with Barclays Bank.

As communications improved, and the size of the malt trade led to road improvements, Hertford's importance increased still further when it became a stage on the main mail-coach route from London to Lincoln, and thus a coaching centre with many inns.

During the 17th century a continuous line of coaching inns stretched from what is now the Post Office in Fore Street, to the Blackbirds—a pub which has had various names, but in a Survey carried out in the reign of James I, was called The Magpie. It has also been known as the Three Blackbirds. An inn called The Chequers occupied part of the present Post Office site.

Another spur to prosperity was the River Lee's improvement for navigation firstly to Ware in 1739, and then to Hertford in 1767. Many of the old maltings and warehouses are sited alongside the Lee Canal.

Open fields surrounded the town until 1803, when the Napoleonic Wars put up the price of corn, and encouraged the owners to enclose them. But the economists reversed the trend in 1846 with the repeal of the Corn Laws.

Another incentive was the opening of the railway to London in 1843 and the growth of commuter traffic. Every population growth since then has coincided with improvement in the rail service. Hertford had a second station at Cowbridge in 1854, which took trains to Welwyn, where passengers changed for London. In 1924, the present North Station was opened, with a direct line to King's Cross. In the 1960s the Hertford/Liverpool Street line was electrified, and the Hertford North line in the 1970s. As a result the population has grown from 15,734 in 1961 to more than 20,000 today.

Industry, if you can call it that, came to Hertford in about 1495, for three years later when Henry VI paid a visit, it boasted what was described as the first fine-paper mill in England, set up by John Tate, son of Sir John Tate, who had been Lord Mayor of London in 1473. The mill is believed to have stood on the site now occupied by Sele Roller Mills in North Road. The king visited the mill again the next year, and records show that on both occasions he gave rewards to Tate.

The book "De Proprietatibus Rerum" of Bartholomaeus Anglicus, printed on the press of Caxton's assistant, Wynkyn de Worde, in 1496, contains the following: "And John Tate the younger Ioye mote he broke whiche late hathe in England doo makes this paper thynne that now in our Englysshe this boke us prynted inne".

Wynkyn de Worde—what an appropriate name for a printer—was a German who was Caxton's works foreman, and when the master died, in 1491, Wynkyn took over the business. There is no evidence that the paper mill existed before 1495, nor after 1507, when Tate senior died.

Hertford had the first gas works in the county, in a street accurately described as Gas House Lane, but now more picturesquely called Marshgate Drive; the works were built by the International Gas Co., in 1825.

Another first was in electricity—the first works in the county was opened in 1900 by the North Metropolitan Electric Power and Distribution Co., Ltd., at Hertford and Barnet.

Hertford had its share of breweries, some of which served the markets, or, from the second half of the 18th century, their own tied houses in a small area. Others served the big houses around the town. There remains McMullens of Hertford.

The plaiting of straw, and straw hat making were a by-product of the wheat growing in the county, but this was mostly a cottage industry. There was a straw hat making business, however, next to the railway bridge on Port Hill, and a sign announcing the fact is still visible on the side of the building.

It was in 1768 that a printer, Stephen Austin, came to the town and founded by far the oldest printing firm still existing in the county. When Haileybury College was founded at Hertford, it was Austin's son who undertook the printing and publishing for the college of oriental texts, and the firm still boasts that it prints in the languages of the world.

Austin started, in 1772, the Hartford Mercury, which after a lapse, became the Hertford Reformer in 1834, and after various changes in title, is now the Hertfordshire Mercury. The firm became associated with Harrison & Sons Ltd., of London in 1909, and was bought by Mr. Peter Fowler in 1972.

In 1827 Peter McMullen operated a small brewery in Railway Street, which he later moved to Mill Bridge. At about the same time John Cater Adams had a brewery at Old Cross, which was acquired in 1852 by William Baker and named the Hope Brewery. In 1920 this was taken over by A. P. and H. McMullen Ltd.

McMullens built a large brewery in Hartham Lane in 1891. It is surmounted by a fine tower, and the clock there is by Moore and Son, Clerkenwell, dated 1829.

Milling was another town trade, and one right by Mill Bridge, demolished in 1967, once bore the legend that a mill had stood on the site for 1,000 years—from the time of the first twin boroughs perhaps? Of the Hertford mills only the Sele Roller Mills remain, and they still make flour.

The mill at Horns Mill turned from milling corn, and then rape, for cake manufacture. It was rebuilt in 1858, but was purchased in 1891 by Webb & Co., leatherdressers, who later specialised in chamois leather, fur-lined gloves. The factory has now been pulled down for housing development.

Hertford also helps to supply London with water, for work was begun in 1608 on the New River, a man-made river which takes water from Chadwell Spring and, since 1738, a measured quantity of water from the River Lee by means of a balance engine or gauge. The gauge now in use was built by William Chadwell Mylne in 1856, and is unique.

The town's fame still rings out all over the country thanks to John Briant, bell founder and clock maker. He came to Hertford in 1780 and his foundry was in Parliament Square, later a printers', and now beautifully restored into offices. In almost 50 years, he cast 422 bells for 185 churches in 16 counties in England, and some for London and Ireland.

His clocks too are famous, and two exist in the town. One is on the Shire Hall, and the other in the tower of All Saints. This one was originally made for St. Mary's, Ware, then went into the workhouse at Kingsmead, and has only recently been installed at All Saints.

Not unnaturally the quest for sand and gravel has played some part in the town's industrial history, and one firm which has been in the business for more than 100 years is H. Brazier Ltd.

Another well-established firm in the town was Creaseys of Hertford Ltd., which had its origins in the 19th century. Robert Creasey, born in 1813, was a tallow chandler, but with the spread of gas lighting, realised there was little future in his trade. He apprenticed his son George to a printer, and in 1885 George set up business in Bull Plain, joined by his own two sons, Horace and Herbert. Herbert was the father of Reginald Creasey, the last head of the firm, which went out of business in the early 1980's.

It was in 1920 that one of the largest employers of labour moved into the town in the shape of Addis Ltd., makers of brushes then, but now of many products manufactured in plastic. The firm had been established in London in 1780.

In 1923 Permanite Ltd., set up a works in Mead Lane as an offshoot of its London factory. They produce roofing and flooring felts of various types. Most of the manufacturing process was transferred to Hertford on the outbreak of the second world war.

A second industrial estate is to be found at Dicker Mill, formerly the mill for the Priory—but Hertford is slowly becoming an office town dominated by County Hall, probably the largest employer. It was not until 50 years after it was established, that the county had permanent central offices in Hertford. Until 1939, departments were scattered around Hertford, and some were in other towns. Some of the county committees actually met in London.

But when Leahoe House, then used as a closed convent, and its surrounding estate came on the market in 1934, it was purchased for £10,000. In the late summer of 1939, with the shadow of the war in the offing, the building was completed. But the hopes of containing all the staff in one building have been frustrated by events, and now they are again spread over the town. Modern extensions have doubled the size of the building. Government offices are housed in Sovereign House, another massive office block completed in the late 1960s.

Left: 13th century corn jar from the Green Dragon Inn site.

Below: Young's Brewery between Brewhouse Lane and South Street. In 1900 Brewhouse Lane was closed and the brewery incorporated in Christ's Hospital.

Above right: Brewer Charles Young (1822-1869).

Above: The Lee navigation, with pleasure boat, and an old warehouse, now demolished to make way for Bircherley Green shopping centre.

Below: the Imperial measures of the Borough of Hertford, 1825.

Above left: Early print of the present McMullen's brewery.

Above right: Peter McMullen, founder of the brewery, 1799-1881.

Below: Chequers yard, demolished in 1890: the property belonged to the Hertford Poor's Estate.

Above: The site of the present post office, and the old Chequers Inn.

Below: Triumphant McMullen workers in procession in about 1912.

THE
HARTFORD MERCURY.

Supplement to the HERTFORDSHIRE MERCURY, Nov. 29, 1884.

Price Two-Pence Halfpenny.]   FRIDAY SEPTEMBER 18, 1772.   N°. 18.

Saturday *and* Sunday's *Posts.*

FOREIGN INTELLIGENCE.

This Day arrived the Mails from Holland and Flanders.

STOCKHOLM, AUGUST 25.

THE King has ordered ten thousand meafures of meal, of twenty pounds each, to be diftributed to the poor.

All the old Senators received their difmiffion on Saturday laft by a note which the King fent to each of them; after which his Majefty nominated fome new Counfellors and Senators, declaring at the fame time that he kept two in *petto.*

The great change in the Government of this kingdom hath been proclaimed (the fame day it was here) at Gothenburgh, Carlfcroon, and many other places; which *proves* that the whole nation unanimoufly wifhed for it. Prince Charles has received the homage of the fubjects in Scania and Gothia, in the fame manner the King has done here; and General Sprengporten is fent into Finland, to receive the oath of fidelity from that province, which is as ready to give it as the others.

The letters of vocation for the new Senators appointed by the King of Sweden were couched, as in the time of Guftavus Adolphus, in thefe words:

"GUSTAVUS, by the Grace of God, King of Sweden, fends greeting: We let you know by thefe prefents, that in confequence of your fidelity, and the diligent fervices which you have in every refpect rendered to us, and the con-

fcription for a new navigable canal from Leeds to Selby, at the King's Arms in this town, on Thurfday laft, the fum of 32,000l. was fubfcribed in lefs than two hours. The faid fubfcription is fince then increafed upwards of 10,000l. and fo fanguine are the wifhes and expectations of the people in general, in regard to its fuccefs, that we are told more money than will be wanted to compleat the fcheme, will be raifed within the limits of our town and neighbourhood.

From the LONDON GAZETTE, *of Saturday, Sept. 12.*

Stockholm, Auguft 25.

THERE has been a Plenum Plenorum this morning, being the firft under the new form of Government. The King's propofitions were read to the States, and confift of four points, all relative to the finances and contributions; and his Majefty demands that they fhould be finifhed in fourteen days, after which the Dyet is to feparate.

As foon as the propofitions were read, all the new Senators, who are in town, took the oaths of their office.

BANKRUPTS.

Robert Bell, of Gravefend, in the county of Kent, Mercer and Draper, to furrender the 10th and 26th of September inftant, at Nine in the forenoon, and the 24th of October next, at Ten in the forenoon, at Guildhall, London. Attorney, Mr. Coore, in Laurence-Pountney-Lane, London.

Jeremiah Dicks, late of Warminfter, in the county of Wilts, Clothier, to furrender the 2d, 3d, and 24th of October next, at Ten in the forenoon, on each of the faid days, at the houfe of Mr. Jofeph Boyter, the Three Lions Inn, in the city of New Sarum.

Above right: The old glove factory at Horns Mill.

Above left: The first Stephen Austin.

Below: Replica of the earliest surviving Hartford Mercury, started in 1772.

Left: The market in Market Place in 1933. It moved here in 1891 when Market Street was built, and closed when the present open market opened in 1934.

Above and centre right: The fulling stocks at the Horns Mill glove factory.

Below right: The balance gauge at the start of the New River.

Above: East Station.

Below: Typical business between the wars—27 Railway Street in 1929.

THE

EASTERN COUNTIES RAILWAY COMPANY

OFFERS THE FOLLOWING ADVANTAGES TO

NERVOUS PERSONS.

Trains at REDUCED SPEED to meet their views

The Rate of Speed is not at all FRIGHTFUL.

For example,—**Hertford** is 21 miles from LONDON by the road,—the time allowed for the second **business** train is **One Hour and Thirty-five Minutes!** *(but the journey is not always accomplished in that time.)* Again,—**Waltham** to LONDON was formerly done in **Thirty-seven Minutes**, the time now allowed is **Fifty-eight Minutes!**

One of the Officials stated that "**The time allowed was so great that they did not know how to kill it!**"

MR. PUNCH says, "The only **Fast** trains on this Line are those that are **Stuck Fast.**" These afford plenty of time for quiet reflection.

N.B.—A person offers for a Wager to run his Donkey against the Train for one stage, and have time for his Breakfast in the bargain ! ! !

The Season Tickets may be 10 or 20 per cent. higher than on other Lines, but as the time allowed for seeing the country is so liberal on the part of the Company, the Passengers must not complain. Railway Companies cannot afford to waste **Time** and **Steam** without being paid for it.

(By Authority)

PASSENGERS.

Commuters in the late 19th century were still dissatisfied, as this poster stuck up by the passengers on the Eastern line, illustrates.

County Hall.

Law and Disorder

Hertford has a long history of local goverment, from the time of William, and when Edward I assigned the castle and town in dower to his second wife, Queen Margaret, he also included an "Honor" which implies a special performance of service to the Crown. Yet it was not until 1925, in the mayoralty of Ald. Josiah Wren, and on his application, that the College of Heralds presented the town with Letters Patent granting the borough a standard, known as the Honor, with the following device: Within a chaplet of roses gules a hart's head caboshed proper between the attires an escoucheon or charged with three chevronells gules."

The chaplet of red roses indicates the borough's connection with the Duchy of Lancaster; and the shield between the hart's antlers has the three red chevrons of the Earls of Hertford and Clare. The standard, of cream silk, was presented to the Corporation in the Castle grounds by the York Herald on October 1, 1925.

The town had had several Royal charters, often confirming each other, and giving authority for the holding of markets. These were all collected up and confirmed in the charter of Queen Mary, dated February 17th, 1554.

Queen Elizabeth I confirmed the charter in 1588, and for the first time the borough was allowed a mace with the royal arms on it, to be carried before the Bailiff in procession.

The charter reduced the number of chief burgesses from 16 to 11, but permitted them to choose sixteen inhabitants to be their assistants. The assistants were elected to the office of chief burgess upon a vacancy, so there was no question of election by the community.

Bailiff and Chief Burgesses were also to elect the Steward of the Town. The first steward under this charter was Robert Spencer, Lord of the Manor of Bengeo. Stewards were replaced by Recorders in 1680.

The charter gave the Corporation the power to make bye-laws, and regularised the existence of the Town Hall which the Corporation had built on the "waste land" in 1555, but for which there had been no royal permission. A gaol was also to be provided.

It was in James I's charter of 1605 that the borough was incorporated under the name of "The Mayor, Burgesses and Commonalty". A High Steward was also to be appointed: the First Earl of Salisbury. Since that time there have only been three High Stewards who were not of this same Cecil family.

Corporation records show that there were many injustices, and the council meetings were often rowdy affairs, with the language far from parliamentary. Councillors attended meetings improperly dressed, and indulged in private feuds. In spite of all this, the Corporation asked, in 1624, for the right to send two members to parliament again, and this was granted. Thomas Fanshaw and William Ashton were elected. Only the freemen of the borough voted in the election.

During the Civil War the Salisburys and Hertford supported the Puritan cause, but Sir

John Harrison of Balls Park and Sir William Cowper, who held the sub lease of Hertford Castle, suffered misfortunes through their support of Charles I.

Rival recruiting officers, in 1642, sought enlistments on both sides, and the town spent money on arms, powder and butts. In the same year the Mayor, Andrew Palmer, and the Steward, John Kelyng, were Royalists, and took strong exception to the drilling of Roundhead men by one of its principal citizens, William Turnor. The names of all involved were taken, and they were charged at Quarter Sessions. When the Grand Jury was assembled it was found, to the great confusion of the Mayor and Steward, that Mr. Turnor was foreman of the jury, which therefore refused to return a "true bill".

Isaac Puller, with strong Puritan sympathies, then trained the Hertford volunteers. Palmer was imprisoned by parliament for reading out a King's Proclamation, and a Roundhead Mayor, Joseph Dalton, appointed. He was later succeeded by "drill sergeant" Puller, to whom the Earl of Salisbury presented a splendid Elizabethan chalice, which is still part of the town's civic plate.

Civil marriages were instituted in 1654, and Corporation and church records show several performed by Puller. The Commonwealth brought other changes. Borough regalia bearing the Royal Cipher or Arms were to be abandoned, and in future all maces were to be made to a uniform pattern and bought from Thomas Maundy. The present Hertford mace has the Maundy stem, but not the head. This was changed in 1660 by Act of Parliament, as the monarchy was restored. The present mace head bears the legend "C.R".

Charles II called in town charters, and substituted new ones. Hertford's extended the borough boundaries considerably. They took in King's Meads, which Charles I sold to the Corporation in 1627, and brought in a large part of the Ware Road and London Road area. A number of changes were also made in the Constitution of the Borough.

Now it was incorporated under the name of Mayor, Aldermen and Commonalty. There were to be 10 Aldermen, one of them being Mayor, and 16 Assistants. A Recorder succeeded the Steward.

The Mayor's right to have a sword as well as a mace carried before him was granted. That sword is still in use. It has a double-edged steel blade, 36 inches long, and bears on both sides the name of "Andreia Ferara" the famous Italian craftsman who made it. The sheath was the gift of Sir Charles Caesar, who gave £100 towards the cost of the charter and the purchase of the sword. Sir Charles, of Benington, represented both the borough and the county in parliament.

The 18th century brought outbreaks of smallpox in the town which seemed to stem from the County Gaol (on the site of the present Corn Exchange, in Fore Street.) It was so bad that people from outside the town were afraid to come in. Others begged to be excused from jury service at assizes because of the "distemper".

There appear to have been three county gaols in Hertford, apart from that at the Castle, which had served so well, but from which people continually escaped. The first was in Back Street (Railway Street) and was a bridewell or house of correction. The one in Fore Street served from about 1702 to 1775, but from then until 1879 it was off Ware Road, on the site of what is now the county's British Red Cross, and Womens Royal Voluntary Service headquarters.

The Fore Street gaol was unsatisfactory from the first, and the new site off Ware Road was bought for £500. The prison cost £6,000 to build, and housed 70 men and 10 women. In 1790 extensions were made to take in the old bridewell.

Beside the gaol, Hertford had a "cage", which housed people detained for offences similar to those for which a night in the cells might now be imposed. Nearby were the whipping post and pillory. All three were immediately east of Market Place. In 1773 they were all moved to The Wash. There was also at one time a ducking stool, on which scolds were dumped in the River Lee, near the Castle Hall.

The gallows were at the top of a long hill, once called Chalk Hill, but now Gallows Hill, on a site opposite the present East Herts Hospital. People from the Fore Street gaol were hanged just opposite, outside the Chequers (now the Talbot Arms).

At the town hall, or sessions house, Assizes and Quarter Sessions were sending people for transportation to the West Indies, the West Coast of Africa, or to Botany Bay. In 1763, for instance, Thomas Whitenail, of Hertford, was transported for seven years for stealing goods worth 4/6d.

Whipping was a common punishment, and one of the most savage recorded was when Rachel, wife of John Bigg, stole two ducks worth 10d. She was whipped from Old Cross through Maidenhead Street to the gaol. The process was repeated two weeks later.

In 1711 Jane Wenham of Walkern was condemned to death for witchcraft, but was reprieved after the kindly judge, Chief Justice Powell, pleaded on her behalf to Queen Anne. She was given a royal pardon and died of old age in Hertingfordbury. Her case caused a pamphlet "war" as a result of which, in 1736 the old laws against witchcraft were repealed.

The present Shire Hall, which was built on the site of the old sessions house, was completed in 1771. The original design was by James Adam, brother of the celebrated Robert Adam. Unfortunately, as so often happens, a committee, and later the county council got at the design and altered it.

At about the same time as the Shire Hall was built records show that elections were lively occasions in the town. There were only 570 electors in 1794, and going to the poll was a farce, and a trial of courage for anyone who wanted to vote, because the election was not secret and there was always the possibility of victimisation afterwards. By the turn of the century it was the "ruffians" of Butchery Green (the shopping centre) who held the key to the Borough seats. The hustings were set up in Market Place, and there was a great competition for window seats in the neighbouring shops. Party agents worked on the Butchery Green residents, and continued to get them tipsy but not drunk—to a point where they just about knew which way to vote. Hertford pubs were listed where drinks could be obtained free, and although the candidates always paid, there was nothing down in writing. Bribery played a major role in the election, and people were even able to obtain houses on a promise of a vote. The elections of 1826, 1830, 1831 and 1832 were probably the most corrupt in the town's history.

Strong arm gangs were also employed ready to lay into people not sporting their party's colours. Whigs and Tories changed seats in this series of elections which led up to the Whig Reform Bill. A Committee of Enquiry into corrupt practices was held at Hertford, and although many of the witnesses were evasive, enough was discovered to prove that voters had been influenced by offers of free food and drink, mostly at The Ship Inn (in Cowbridge) and "The Woolpack". There was evidence that the Tory supporters hired "bullies", and quartered them in strategic places in the town, and various other acts of corruption were proved. As a result the two Tory members, Lord Mahon and Lord Ingestre were deprived of their seats, and from 1832 to 1835 the borough had no members.

By the second Reform Bill, Hertford was reduced to a single member, and attention was then turned to reform of the boroughs. Commissioners examined Hertford's record in December 1833. The corporation did not accept the legality of the commission, and a protest was read out by the Town Clerk, Mr. Philip Longmore, when the commission opened its first session, but he added that as the corporation had nothing to hide, it was prepared to give every assistance to the commissioners.

In the event the corporation came out very much on the right side, one of the commissioners writing: "I have visited many Corporations in England, and through the whole course of my experience, I have seen no instance in which a Corporation has taken so much pains to record their acts as in this, or where they have displayed so much labour in openly and fully disclosing their conduct."

It was the Municipal Corporations Act of 1835 that introduced the elective principle into local government. Hertford lost its Recorder and individual Quarter Sessions. This form of local government existed in the town until April 1974, when the borough became incorporated into East Herts District Council, on which it has 11 members. After several attempts the town decided to retain its town council, but its powers are now limited to those of a parish council.

To commemorate the Coronation of King George VI, the town was granted "supporters" for the Coat of Arms; two lions ermine, gorged in red now support the shield with the traditional hart lodged in water. The motto is "Pride in our Past, Faith in our Future".

Of the public buildings in the town, the Corn Exchange was built in 1858, moving the corn market from underneath the Shire Hall arches. Now the hall has been split into shops with a first floor multi-purpose hall. At one time it housed the town's library, until that was moved to a new building, erected to celebrate the jubilee of Queen Victoria, at Old Cross.

The County Hospital in North Road was extended and rebuilt in 1923, and in 1973 a twin operating theatre, described as one of the finest and most up-to-date in Eastern England, was added. The hospital itself was built in 1833. East Herts Hospital was built later as an isolation hospital, as well as still being used for post-operative cases from the County Hospital, it houses the headquarters of East Herts Health Authority, and Seward Lodge, a pioneer unit for elderly, mentally handicapped patients.

Bull Plain, in which the market was once held, also boasts Lombard House, now the Hertford Club. This is an early 17th century building which overhangs the river but is part of a medieaval hall house. It was once the home of Sir Henry Chauncy, who wrote a history of the county, and it used to house judges. Also in Bull Plain is the town's museum.

Hertford's war memorial in Parliament Square is one of the finest in the country. It is surmounted by a hart, and was designed by Sir Aston Webb. The site was given by the late Sir Edward and Lady Pearson.

St Andrew Street in the late 18th century.

The charter of James I which gave the town its first mayor.

The charter of Charles I.

94

Below: Charles II.

Above: Charles II's charter.

Above: The mayor's chain surrounds the badges of office used on less formal occasions by the mayor (left) and the mayoress. Beneath is the ceremonial sword, and below that the mace.

Below: The Honor of Hertford.

96

Above: On October 1 1925, the Mayor, Ald Josiah Wren receives the Honor from the York Herald. On the left, in uniform is the Marquess of Salisbury, and on the right, the Marchioness.

Below: Print of Fore Street at the end of the 18th century, showing the gaol entrance on the right next to the Cross Keys inn. The newly built Shire Hall had not suffered later alterations.

Above: On January 9, 1824 John Thurtell of Hertford, was hanged outside the Baker Street gaol for the murder of Mr William Weare at Elstree.

Below: The gallows from Hertford gaol were removed in 1878, and are now in the Chamber of Horrors at Madame Tussaud's.

Above: The old Sessions House, which made way for the Shire Hall in 1769. An Elizabeth building, it was suggested by one leading citizen that "the new hall should be built of the material from the old" but the old hall should be used until the new one was built!

Below: The White Hart, one of Hertford's oldest pubs.

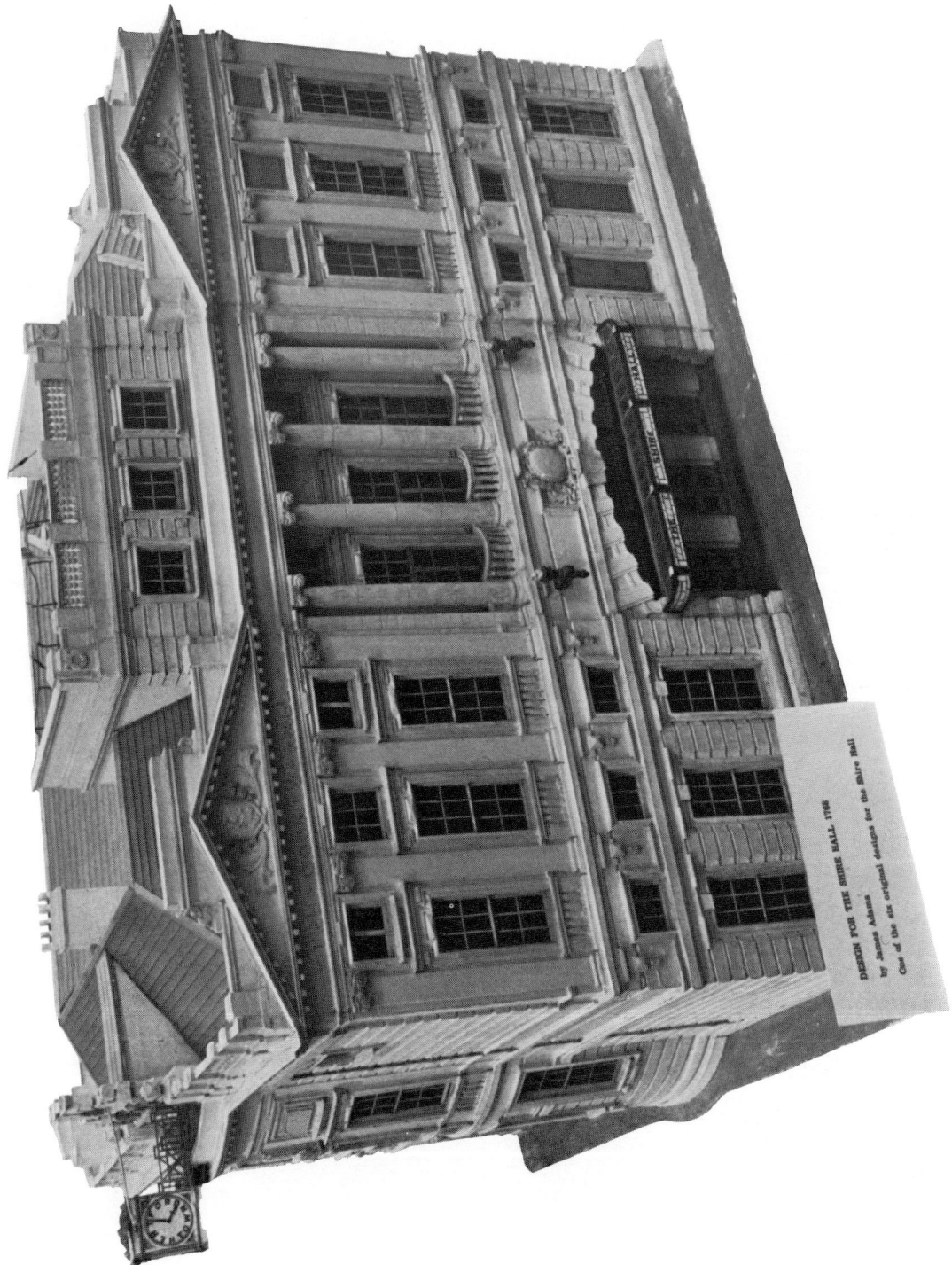

James Adam's model of what the Shire Hall should have looked like, based on his own plans.

The Shire Hall as it was before large internal and some external alterations carried out in 1987/8.

101

Above: The old Corn Exchange, built on the site of one of Hertford's gaols, but replaced in 1858.

Below: The opening of the Free Public Library by the Hon. A. J. Balfour, Hertford's MP, in 1888. Ald A. P. McMullen was the mayor.

Above: The Corn Exchange before alterations, with Hertford Dramatic and
Operatic Society's pantomime "Cinderella" being advertised.

Below: The last Hertford Borough Council, pictured only days before it was
swallowed up by East Herts District Council. With the mayor, Ald Tony Bentley,
is the Bishop of Hertford, the Rt. Rev. Peter Mumford.

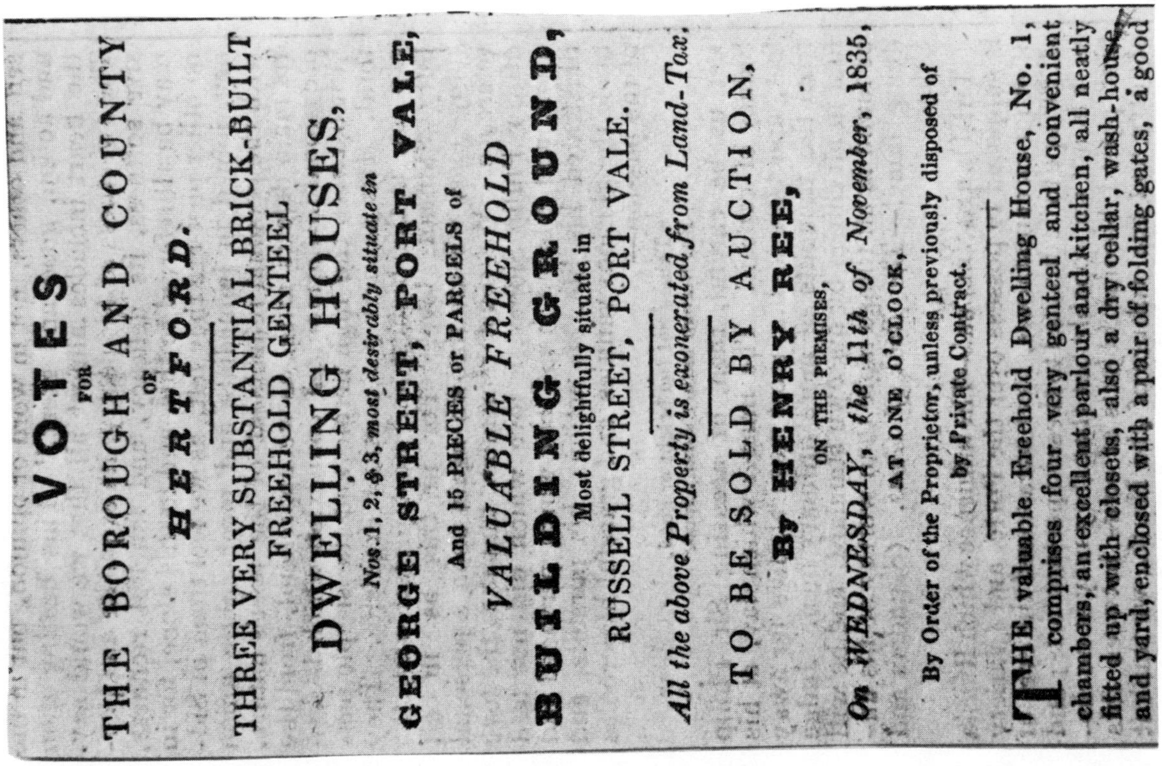

VOTES
FOR
THE BOROUGH AND COUNTY
OF
HERTFORD.

THREE VERY SUBSTANTIAL BRICK-BUILT
FREEHOLD GENTEEL
DWELLING HOUSES,
Nos. 1, 2, & 3, most desirably situate in
GEORGE STREET, PORT VALE,
And 15 PIECES or PARCELS of
VALUABLE FREEHOLD
BUILDING GROUND,
Most delightfully situate in
RUSSELL STREET, PORT VALE.

All the above Property is exonerated from Land-Tax.

TO BE SOLD BY AUCTION,
By HENRY REE,
ON THE PREMISES,
On WEDNESDAY, the 11th of November, 1835,
AT ONE O'CLOCK,
By Order of the Proprietor, unless previously disposed of
by Private Contract.

THE valuable Freehold Dwelling House, No. 1, comprises four very genteel and convenient chambers, an excellent parlour and kitchen, all neatly fitted up with closets, also a dry cellar, wash-house and yard, enclosed with a pair of folding gates, a good

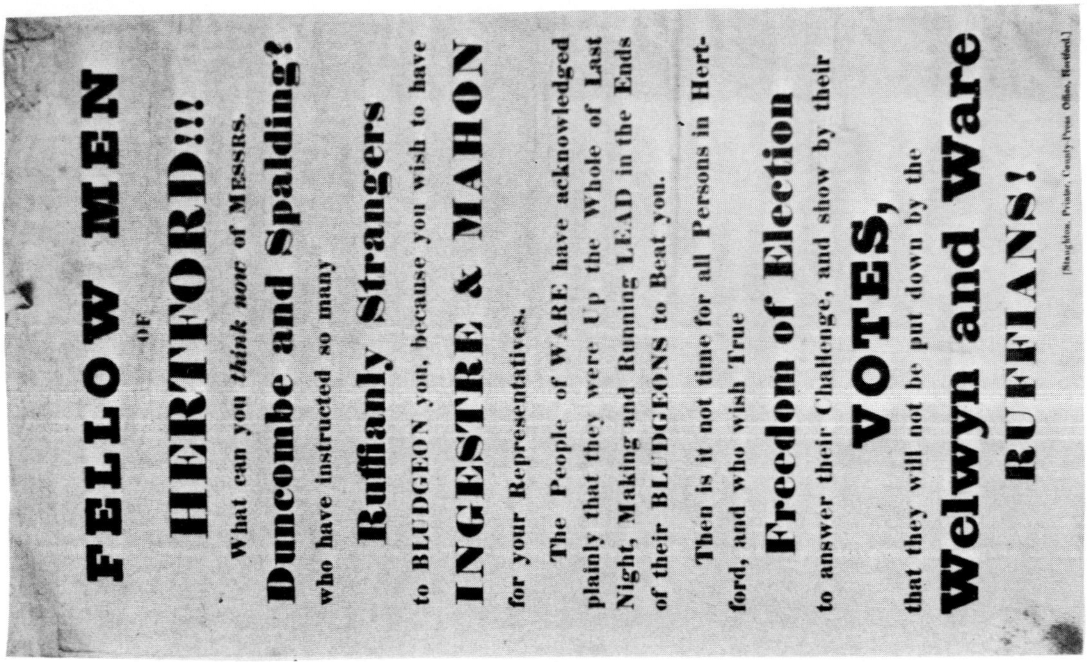

FELLOW MEN
OF
HERTFORD!!!

What can you think now of MESSRS.
Duncombe and Spalding?
who have instructed so many
Ruffianly Strangers
to BLUDGEON you, because you wish to have
INGESTRE & MAHON
for your Representatives.

The People of WARE have acknowledged plainly that they were Up the Whole of Last Night, Making and Running LEAD in the Ends of their BLUDGEONS to Beat you.

Then is it not time for all Persons in Hertford, and who wish True
Freedom of Election
to answer their Challenge, and show by their
VOTES,
that they will not be put down by the
Welwyn and Ware
RUFFIANS!

[Slaughton, Printer, County Press Office, Hertford.]

Above: Typical advertisement of the times (1835); houses for votes.

Below: It took a brave man to vote in the election of 1832.

Above: The old toll house on Mill Bridge.

Below: Hertford Museum, a 17th century house improved in the 18th century, and converted into a museum by R. T. and W. F. Andrews in 1914. The last occupier of the house was T. Pamphillon, a plumber, and captain of Hertford Fire Brigade.

105

Hertford Fire Brigade, 1887-1898.

The Gain of Learning

It was in the 14th year of the reign of James I (1617) that letters patent were granted to Richard Hale, of Cheshunt, to found a grammar school for boys in the town. His reason for building it at Hertford and not at Cheshunt was "because of the pure air, so that parents need have no fear for their children's loss of health for the gain of learning".

Before his death in 1620, Richard Hale put up a brick building on the edge of All Saints' Churchyard. It is still there, although enlarged, has been an annexe of the new Simon Balle School, and is now the East Herts Divisional Schools Library centre, and an in-service training centre for teachers.

A house was purchased in Fore Street for the master, but at the beginning of this century Bayley Hall was bought for him, and the whole school was repaired and expanded. So it went on as a public secondary school for boys until 1930 when the county council built a new school on a site off Peg's Lane into which Hale's foundation was merged.

The school was known as Hertford Grammar School for Boys, and former Hale pupils were known as "Hale's Foundationers". But the name soon lapsed. With yet another change in educational thinking, it has now again become the Richard Hale School.

One major educational foundation which had its buildings in the town until 1985 — Christ's Hospital School — was founded by Edward VI in London in 1546, on the site of the Grey Friars' premises sacked by his father, Henry VIII. From those early days, many of the youngsters were sent to Hertford and other towns and villages in the area, for special care. Their uniform entitled them to be called Blue Coats.

Circa 1694, 20 cottages arranged in parallel lines of ten were built. Each was occupied by a tenant nurse, who paid rent to the hospital, and in return boarded and catered for 20 children for an agreed sum.

The writing school was at the far end of the playground, and became the school hall. Until 1783 it was the only school house, but the grammar school, on the right of the entrance gates was built in 1783. This is now the headmistress's house.

In addition to 20 nurses for the boys, there were at least two for the girls. The whole of the girls' school was moved from London to Hertford in 1778. The original school is the line of buildings facing Fore Street, with the figures of two girls wearing the dress of that time. The main gates, with the figures of two boys in their blue coats, were presented by a prominent Hertford doctor, Sir John Dimsdale junior in about 1721.

It is said that the figures of the boys were erected soon after one boy had been murdered at the school by another. The story goes that the murderer was hanged at Hertford Gaol, and the dead boy buried in All Saints. One of the figures faces the old gaol area, the other looks towards All Saints.

The boys were eventually moved to Horsham in 1902, and the school's splendid buildings

107

were opened, as a modern girls' school in 1906 by the Prince and Princess of Wales; in 1928 the Princess Mary, Viscountess Lascelles opened further buildings. The girls moved to Horsham in 1985, and the site now houses offices and dwellings.

The Green Coat School was one of a number set up by Gabriel Newton, an alderman of the borough of Leicester, in about 1762. But it was not until 1812 that a school house was built on the north side of All Saints churchyard. That same building housed a chapel of rest, but is now a house. There was also a Green Coat school for girls, but there are scant records of this. It continued until about 1788 when it first closed, and then was rescued by Baroness Dimsdale.

Hertford's Green Coat School moved into new buildings in London Road in 1867, but by 1870, when the first General Education Act came in, it was unable to compete with the new subsidised primary schools. It now no longer exists as a school.

In 1811 the Hertford National School "for the education of boys in the principles of the Established Church," was started for 100 pupils in a school house on a piece of ground bordering the Castle walls.

Lord Salisbury had resumed possession of the land by 1842, and the children taught at the school were absorbed into the Cowper Memorial School, built in London Road in 1841. In 1846 All Saints' Infant School was established by public subscription, and by the same means Bengeo Church of England School was founded before 1850 and St. Andrew's Church of England School in 1875. A girls' school was added at Bengeo in 1860, and in 1861 the Abel Smith Memorial School for Girls was built.

St. Andrew's school has been transferred to the town's Sele Farm Estate, while the Bengeo school has been pulled down, and transferred to a site on the edge of the town, near the Molewood Estate. A new primary school, Hollybush is also at Sele Farm. Of the older schools in the town, the Port Vale school is now Millmead School and was built by the county council in 1915, as was a mixed school in Morgans Walk. About 60 years ago St. Joseph's Convent School was established at St. John's Street, opposite the Roman Catholic church. It moved in the late 1950s to Hertingfordbury, while the parish school, founded in 1883, is in new premises in North Road.

A School of Industry was established in the town in 1793 by three women of the Society of Friends, but although Turnor mentions it in his 1830 history, little is known subsequently.

In 1691 Hertfordshire Quakers reported to the yearly meeting that they had two schools in Hertford. Christopher Taylor, later prominent in the Quaker colony of Pennsylvania was a schoolmaster in Hertford in the late 1660s. There was also a Dame school in Hertford, in a house in Ware Road, which still has the figures of two dogs on each side of the path leading to the front door.

The British and Foreign Schools Society had a school near Cowbridge, in the early part of the 19th century, catering for non-conformist children, later taken over by the county council as a school for girls and infants. Much later it was an annexe for the Hertford Secondary School.

After the Indian Mutiny, the East India Company for whose service Haileybury College trained young men, was wound up. The buildings fell into disrepair, and the 400 acres of grounds were unused. However, in 1820 Stephen Austin (III) suggested that the buildings should be turned into a public school. Two years later a royal charter was granted, and Haileybury has become one of the best known schools of its kind.

The original Haileybury buildings were designed by William Wilkins, architect of the National Gallery in London. The domed chapel was added in 1876. Sixteen of its former pupils won the Victoria Cross, two the George Cross, and 156 have become generals. Earl Attlee, prime minister from 1945 to 1951, was a pupil.

Above left: Christ's Hospital School at the end of the 18th century.

Below left: Although the school has left, the boys are still there. They are replicas of the originals which have gone to Horsham.

Right: Close-ups of the boys in their blue-coat uniform.

Tht boys at Christ's Hospital in 1902.

The girls' traditional costume at Christ's Hospital.

Right: The original Green Coats School building, as a mortuary.

Left: A bust of Henry Cowper, in whose memory Cowper school was built in 1841.

Above: The Tower School was held in this building in the Castle wall. St Andrew Church is in the background. The print is dated 1776.

Below: The original Hale Grammar School, from a print dated 1860. The building still stands just off All Saints churchyard.

112

Above: The present Richard Hale School.

Below: Haileybury College in about 1908.

East India College students at Hertford Castle: a print which probably shows an architect's view of what his expensive plans would have made of the Castle.

Into Battle

Due to the Castle, Hertford has a reputation for fighting for good causes, or causes that seemed to be good at the time. How much fighting was done by the able-bodied men of the town before 959 is impossible to say, but King Edgar decreed that each area, called a Hundred, had to provide fully armed soldiers in time of national danger, and Hertford was one of the Hundreds in the county to provide men.

Hertford men must have been involved in defending the Castle against the Dauphin of France, and the county frequently furnished companies of Yeomen and Archers for foreign service at the time of Crecy and Poitiers during the Hundred Years' War.

In Tudor times the county provided quotas of Militia in national crises, and when Princess Elizabeth, by order of her sister, Queen Mary, was taken from Hertford Castle to Hatfield, she was escorted by a Troop of Hertfordshire Horse Militia. The Hertfordshire Muskets in the time of Elizabeth was particularly commended for efficiency, served in France, Holland and Ireland, and was frequently selected as the Queen's private bodyguard.

During the Civil War the county's sympathy lay mainly with Parliament, and it was the predominant partner in Cromwell's Eastern Association. It was at Hertford that Cromwell quelled a mutiny in his ranks on November 15, 1647. One third of his army was ordered to meet at Cockbush Field—a site just off the present Ware Road, about a mile from the town centre. Plots were afoot, and Cromwell and General Fairfax made their headquarters at Hertford on November 13 and 14, probably at the Bell (now the Salisbury Arms).

The conspirators' plan was to hold Fairfax on his arrival at Hertford. Cromwell was to be shot in his bed on the Sunday night.

The trouble was that apart from the regiments ordered by Cromwell to be at Hertford, two mutinous regiments led by Lilburn and Harrison were also marching to the rendezvous. Lilburn's regiment was known as the "Levellers", and had mutinied against its officers. They believed "all degrees of men should be levelled, and an equality established both in titles and estates throughout the kingdom."

When Cromwell and Fairfax arrived at Cockbush Field a strange sight met their eyes. Lilburn's and Harrison's regiments had papers stuck in their hats which read "England's freedom and soldiers' rights". They were repeatedly told to remove the slogans, without effect. Another regiment thrust its leaders to the front with a petition for "The agreement of the people", but the "Levellers" were in the eye of the storm.

Cromwell eventually lost his temper, drew his pistol, and ran at the mutineers, knocking two or three on the head. This stormy action suddenly cowed the men, and they took the paper from their hats and begged for mercy.

A Council of War was held on the spot, and 11 of the mutineers were called out of the ranks. Three of them were tried and condemned to death, but they were allowed to gamble on which of them would suffer the extreme penalty. Dice were thrown, and a man named Arnald was shot at the head of the regiment. He became a martyr to the "Levellers".

Hertford was almost blown up during the Civil War. An order by the House of Commons ruled that the magazine was in a dangerous place, so it was moved to the town hall—on the site of the present Shire Hall.

A news-letter printed in London (they were the newspapers of the time) led its front page "Terrible newes from Hartford! Discovering the manner how the town was set on fire!" The story told "that the towne of Hartford was on Friday the 12th of this month (August 1642) set on fire by means of a villan that threw a ball of wild fire into a brewhouse which burnt it down with divers other houses, who presently fled away". It appears the magazine was housed nearby.

After the austerities of the Protectorate, the Restoration was proclaimed with great jollifications. The cost to Hertford was as follows: "For proclaiming the King 4s; for the ringers, 5s; for soldiers and bonfires, 9s 6d; the Arms of the Commonwealth to be taken down and the King's Arms put up."

Now the king set about raising the country's first professional army. In 1683, on his orders, the 1st Dragoons ("The Royals"), were formed from four disbanded troops of the Tangiers Light Horse, and two troops raised in Hertfordshire. One of these was raised at Hertford itself by Viscount Cornbury, son of the Earl of Clarendon.

But on every subsequent occasion or threat of war, volunteer troops were formed, mostly by leading county families. In addition, Hertfordshire had to provide 116 men for the navy in 1795. In 1798, when the Volunteers were raised (known locally as the "Hartford Association of Gentlemen"), colours were presented at All Saints' Church. The town raised a further company of Hertford Volunteers under Captain the Hon. E. Spencer Cowper, when Bonaparte threatened to invade. The town celebrated Nelson's victory at Trafalgar, and the Militia and volunteer units were disbanded but the Yeomanry was retained.

By 1831 the South Herts Yeomanry had four troops, one of which was split between Hertford and Hoddesdon. In 1900 the Yeomans saw their first active service abroad, in the South African Campaign.

The Militia had been reconstituted by the time the Crimean War broke out (1854-56). By 1859 a war with France seemed possible and a Volunteer Rifle Corps, in addition to the Militia, was called for. In 1873 the headquarters of the Militia, which had been at Hatfield, was moved to Hertford in inadequate quarters at Railway Street—then Back Street. The government then changed the name of the Hertfordshire Militia to the 4th Battalion of the Bedfordshire Regiment, and it stayed that way for 27 years. A move to make headquarters at Bedford was mooted. Questions were asked in Parliament; the corporation under the Mayor, Dr John Tasker Evans, raised £6,000 to build a barracks on land behind The Plough Inn, and despite War Office obstruction, the barracks were built.

Men of the 4th Battalion saw service in South Africa, and Pte. Martin-Leake, of High Cross, won the VC at Vlakfontein. As an officer in the RAMC he won a clasp to the decoration in 1914 in the Zennebeke campaign.

On the army's reorganisation in 1908, the Territorials was formed, and the Hertfordshire Regiment was created, the 1st Bn. of which was presented with colours bearing the badge of the hart lodged in water, by King Edward VII at Windsor in 1909.

At the outbreak of World War I, the county had the 1st Bn. the Hertfordshire Regiment under Lieut-Col. Viscount Hampden, the 270th Bde. Royal Field Artillery, and the Hertford-

116

shire Yeomanry. Of the artillery, "A" battery was based on Hertford. The Hertfordshire Regiment was among the first Territorial units to arrive in France, and went into action November 11, 1914, continuing to serve until November 11, 1918. It won the reputation of having never lost a trench. Two men of the Regiment won VCs: Cpl A. Burt, from Hertford in 1915, and Second Lt. F. E. Young was posthumously awarded the second at Havrincourt in 1918.

The Yeomanry first went to Egypt for the defence of the Suez Canal, and then to Gallipoli after the Suvla Bay landings. After evacuation from Gallipoli they returned to Egypt for a campaign against the Senussi Arabs, German allies. The Yeomanry was then split up to serve with infantry divisions. "B" squadron—the Hertford section—went to France and fought on the Somme, Thiepval, Ancre, and Arras. They then returned to Egypt for a period in the Cavalry School at Zeitoun. In May, 1918 the squadron went to Palestine to join the Hertford "A" battery of the 270th Brigade RFA, and took part in the pursuit of the Turks from Megiddo to Haifa, Acre, Tyre, Beirut and Tripoli.

"A" Battery had a frustrating war. It was not until November that it received orders to go to France, and then to Egypt, where, some members claimed, they were treated as camels, hauling horse artillery in the cloying and shifting sands of the desert. However, in 1917, the battery took part in the invasion of Palestine, fighting in the three battles of Gaza.

The town itself suffered from war. As early as October 1915 there was a Zeppelin raid which destroyed houses in North Road, and nine people were killed and 20 injured when bombs dropped in Bull Plain, near Lombard House. Elderly residents claim that 40 small bombs were dropped on the town in under two minutes. A Zeppelin passed over the town again in 1916, to be shot down at Cuffley, and in 1917 bombs were dropped on Queen's Hill.

In the second world war Hertfordshire had more bombs to the acre than any county in England, and the county town had its share.

For some strange reason it was decided, against the advice of the Corporation, to evacuate some of London's children to the town. Early on a landmine killed people in Tamworth Road, and other bombs dropped without causing casualties. Throughout the war the ARP with its headquarters at The Wash was kept constantly on the alert. The town also had its Home Guard, and Observer Corps.

The Territorial Army was also ready; Hertfordshire Regiment under Lieut-Col. John Longmore was the first county regiment to complete its second line unit, the 1st Bn. being recruited on the Hertford side of the county. The Hertford Battery, 342, of the 86th Field Regiment Royal Artillery, was also ready, and together they helped to form the 54th East Anglian Division. Yet the 1st Bn. was kept at home until 1943 when it was sent for garrison duty to Gibraltar. It went onto Italy with the Fifth Army, in its assault on the Gothic Line.

The battery was first on anti-invasion duties, and in 1943 was one of the first to be equipped with self-propelling field guns. The battery took part in the D-Day landings, in support of the 50th Northumbrian Infantry at La Riviere. Henceforth it stayed with the 21st Army Group in almost continuous action until VE Day.

In 1946 the Regiment, as well as the Territorial Army, was disbanded, but was reconstituted in 1947. The artillery was moved to St. Albans. Colours of the regiment were laid up in All Saints Church, Queen Elizabeth, the Queen Mother, a popular visitor to the town, doing the honours. She was Honorary Colonel of the regiment. The borough paid its tribute in 1954 when the regiment was presented with the Freedom of the town.

Cromwell quells the "Levellers" rebellion at Cockbush Field—a print
hitherto unknown.

Above left: Oliver Cromwell.

Above right: The present day Salisbury Arms Hotel, formerly known as The Bell.

Below: An early picture of the Hertford Militia Band.

Left: Mr T. J. Sworder, town clerk in 1878/79, and from 1894 to 1912,
in the undress uniform of the 1st (Hertfordshire) Vol. Bn. of the Beds Regiment.

Right: Mr Henry Shephard in the band sergeant's full dress uniform (walking out)
of the 1st (Hertfordshire) Vol. Bn. of the Beds Regiment.

Above: Taken at camp in 1895—a group of the 1st (Hertfordshire) Vol. Bn. of the Beds Regiment. Left to right: B. J. Gripper, Fred Fountain, Leonard McMullen, and Herbert Baker, later to become the first fully-fledged bell-ringing mayor of Hertford.

Below: After Zeppelin bombs had struck in Bull Plain on October 13, 1915, in the background is the elegant Lombard House.

121

Above right: Parliament Row, probably about 1922. It was demolished that year to make way for the town's war memorial. The third building on the right is the present Blackbirds pub.

Above left: The war memorial. The building to the right is now the social services office of the County Council, but it was originally John Briant's bell foundry.

Below: Hertford Motor Company pictured when serving as a British Restaurant during the 1939-45 war. It has now been demolished to make way for a Bejam freezer centre.

Above: V bomb damage in 1945. It demolished Wickham's brewery and the
brewery tap, and also part of Ilott's Mill, at Mill Bridge.
Mr Illott can be seen surveying the damage.

Below: Quiet corner of St Andrew Street, with the 16th century verger's house,
now an antique shop, on the right, At the far end of the left hand side of the street
is the HQ of the 5th Company of the 5th (Hertfordshire) Bn., of the
Royal Anglian Regiment.

Richard Westall's painting "Harvest Storm", which hangs in the Shire Hall.

A Peal of People

The story of Hertford is eventually the story of the people—the landowners and the civic leaders; the builders and the destroyers; the famous and the curious. Bellmaker Briant, generous to a fault, died at 81 in 1829 worth little. Because All Saints had eight splendid bells from 1674, bellringing has been popular in the town, and in 1767 the Hertford College Youths was founded. The name goes back to Sir Richard Whittington (Dick Whittington) Lord Mayor of London, who in 1637 built a college close to an old church, and the youths of the college used to practice ringing. In the same year the Society of College Youths was founded in London. In the early part of the 18th century, the Society would ring at Hertford, and encouraged the Hertford bell ringers to adopt a similar name.

The rules provided for the annual election of a master, and among them have been Baron Dimsdale (1781), Lord Fairford (1782) and in 1907, Mr Herbert Baker, master in the same year that he was mayor. During his year of office he took part in a peal of 5040 changes of Stedman Triples on the bells of All Saints, being the first mayor to ring a peal.

The ringers were governed by strict rules, and any not attending the Thursday practices were fined 2d. Ringers were not allowed to leave practice without the consent of the other ringers, and if they did, a similar fine was imposed. These went towards paying for the annual feast, held in a local inn. In 1773 William Hillier was suspended for ill-treating fellow ringers. He made a public apology and was reinstated, but was warned that if it happened again he would be expelled.

The society went into suspended animation in 1822, and when, in 1876 St Andrew's Bells were rehung in the new tower, a new society known as The Hertford Change Ringers was formed. But in 1879, when they were publicly recognised as the ringing society of the town, they adopted the title still held today: Hertford College Youths Society of Change Ringers. Since then the society has been responsible for ringing the bells of both All Saints and St Andrew.

Mention of Baron Dimsdale brings us to one of Hertford's most famous inhabitants, who set up practice in the town in 1734 as Dr Thomas Dimsdale. A restless man, who sought excitement and change, he joined up as medical officer to the Duke of Cumberland's army going north to fight Bonny Prince Charlie. Then he became interested in innoculation against smallpox, and against great opposition which at one time nearly drove him from his profession, he continued with experiments which in 1767 resulted in a book on the subject which aroused world-wide interest.

In the following year the Czarina Catherine the Great of Russia invited him to St Petersburg to innoculate her and the Czarevitch Paul. It was a risky business, and the Czarina arranged that in the event of her death, a coach and relay of horses should be available to give him a quick and safe exit from the country.

The innoculations were a success, and Dimsdale, with his son Nathaniel returned to Hertford, both created hereditary barons of the Russian Empire. He also received £12,000 and a £500 annuity. The Russian court wanted him to settle in Russia, but although he went back in 1781 to innoculate other members of the Romanov family, he returned to Hertford determined to set up a clinic for poor patients, and innoculated people from all over this country as well as visitors from overseas. He died in 1800 at the age of nearly 90, and was buried in the Quaker cemetery at Bishop's Stortford. There is no memorial to him in the town, although a public house in Fore Street bears his name, as did a house in Bull Plain, recently restored, but renamed Beadle House.

Samuel Stone, joint founder of the town of Hartford, Connecticut, lived in Hertford, England. The facts are these: John Stone lived, according to surveys of 1621, 1628 and 1631, in a house adjoining the Redd Lion Inn in Fore Street. This is now the site of Barclays Bank. He had a large family, of whom Samuel was the third child. Samuel was baptised at All Saints' Church, on July 30 1602. It is believed that John was one of the borough assistants, for in the Month's Court Minutes, dated October 4 1637, he is deprived of his office for being absent from the borough for a year. During that time he and his family had "lately gone beyond the seas and hath there seated and planted himselfe and his ffamilye and doth there intend to resyde and dwell." Samuel Stone sailed, in 1633, in the Ship Griffin with Thomas Hooker and John Cotton, and in 1636 assisted in founding the American Hartford. One can only speculate that his father joined him with the rest of his family.

Another man of his times was John Finch, who was mayor in 1626-27. It was during his mayoralty that the Corporation purchased Hartham (still a fine open space for recreation) and Kings Meads, together with a considerable amount of property and rights, from King Charles I, for £100.

He was a strongwilled man, for the Month's Court Minutes later show him to have been fined on a number of occasions for failure to attend at the Month's Court. On April 28 1629, when sent for he "did absolutely refuse to come" and on April 28 he again refused "being at the Green Dragon (opposite the old John Briant's works) at Table with a stranger." Yet he appears to have been knighted in 1630, for the records then show him as Sir John Finch.

In 1621 a survey of the borough was made, remembering that the borough boundary was much smaller than it is today, (as Speed's map of the time shows), but there were 25 inns and alchouses here. Seven still occupy their same or nearby sites, but only one, the White Hart, has the nearest approximation to its 1621 name White Hearts.

Of the others, Chequers was on part of the present Talbot Arms site; Redd Lion is now Dimsdale Arms; Bell—Salisbury Arms; Magpie—Blackbirds; Black Lyon—Three Tuns; the Green Dragon retains its original site, but was a bonded warehouse for some years.

The others were Falcon, Angel, Naked Boy, Bull, Kings Head, George, Hoggshills, Kings Arms, Rose, Labour in Vain, Swan, Cross Keys, Horseshoe, Prince's Arms, Glove, Catherine Wheel, Maidenhead, and Cressant. Of these the Labour in Vain (later the Red Cow) closed in 1910, the Maidenhead went in 1933, and the Rose (later the Old Coffee House) closed in 1938.

It is strange that the only Radical MP the town ever returned, Thomas Slingsby Duncombe (1826-31), has a public house named after him in Railway Street. In fact the Dimsdale Arms was originally the Duncombe Arms, but when it was bought by the Dimsdale family it clearly could not still bear the name of a political rival!

Other notable M.P.s of the borough include Sir William Cowper, who lived at Hertford

Castle, became Lord Chancellor, and later Earl Cowper for his services to Queen Anne in trying to bring about the union of England and Scotland in 1706. On the Queen's death he was nominated one of the lords justices of the kingdom for carrying on government until the arrival of George I. Arthur James Balfour, afterwards Earl Balfour, with a later Earl Cowper, presented the borough with the Mayor's chain and badge in 1880. A leader in his field, Mr. F. W. Dodderidge, in 1940 restored the pargetting in Market Place. He has left his mark on the town as surely as others of more exalted rank. Artist Richard Westall was born at Hertford in 1765, in a house in West Street. In 1779 he was apprenticed to an heraldic engraver in Gutter Lane, Cheapside. He studied at an evening school of art, and had a portrait-drawing exhibited in the Royal Academy in 1784. He was admitted a student there the next year. He became an associate in 1792, and an academician in 1794. He illustrated many books of the period, but he was best in watercolour, and was the leader of a reform in figure-painting. In his later years he lost most of his earnings by imprudent dealings in old pictures and other speculations, and had to receive relief from the Royal Academy. He and his blind sister were also assisted by the Duchess of Kent. Westall's last professional occupation was as instructor in painting and drawing to Princess Victoria. He died on December 4th, 1836.

His younger brother William was born at Hertford on October 12th, 1781. He was a topographical painter, and was appointed landscape draughtsman for an exploration expedition in Australia. William died in 1850.

What about the women? Mrs. Robert Addis was the first woman to be elected to the borough council in 1932, later becoming the first woman alderman in 1940, but the first woman mayor was Mrs. Winifred Brooks, who held the office in 1957. She has since been made a Freeman of the Borough. Her late husband, Ald. Percy Brooks was mayor in 1945-46 and 1953-54. First woman chairman of the bench was Ald. Mrs. M. H. Purkiss-Ginn, of the family which has had such an influence on the town.

The freedom of the town has been given sparingly—and only comparatively recently to people who lived in the town. The Duke of Wellington received the freedom before Waterloo, which meant that afterwards the borough had shot its bolt as far as honours were concerned.

Sir George Faudel-Phillips of Ball's Park was made a freeman in 1897, and Sir Edward and Lady Pearson, of Brickendonbury in 1922. Mr. Philip Raynsford Longmore, who gave the Warren to the town, was granted a freedom in 1935, and in 1954 the freedom was granted to the Hertfordshire Regiment.

Ald. Alexander Purkiss Ginn was granted his freedom in 1929 after almost a life time's service to the town. He had been mayor on four occasions, and served the council as auditor, councillor and alderman for over 40 years. He first pulled the switch which lit the town with electricity; he helped promote the town's sewage works, and helped to secure the reconstruction of the Mill Bridge.

A man of humble beginnings, now considered the first "working man" to gain the freedom, Ald. George Mansfield, printer from Bengeo, worked hard for the town; he was twice mayor—1938-39, and 1940 on the death of Ald. Ashley Webb during his year of office.

Then there are the Andrews brothers. Ald. W. F. Andrews did much for All Saints Church and gave the alabaster reredos to the new church; he was mayor three times. With his brother, R. T. Andrews, he founded the Museum.

We must never forget the unnamed man who, in the autumn of 1762 announced by public notice that he would "fly" from the tower of All Saints Church. He thrilled hundreds of people. He stretched a rope from the top of the tower to the ground where it was drawn over two strong pieces of wood nailed across each other. This was then fastened to a stake driven into the ground. Two or three feather beds were then placed upon the cross timbers. The man had a flat board with a groove in the middle of it which he attached to his chest. He then lay on the top of the rope, heading downwards, and adjusted the rope into the groove in the board. Properly balanced, he "flew" to the ground onto the feather beds. But he had problems. He had lost one leg and had a wooden substitute. In order to balance himself he filled the wooden leg with lead. Three times he "flew". The second time he blew a trumpet on the way down, and the third time had a pistol in each hand, firing them as he descended!

Hertford Dramatic and Operatic Society is more than 60 years old, but Hertford Castle in about 1430 saw the early dawning of drama in an entertainment presented before Henry VI at Christmas. It was by John Lydgate, a monk at Bury St Edmunds, and was described as "a disguising for the King holding his noble feest of Cristmas in the Castel of Hartford". It had, unusually for the time, three speakers, and was the first recorded instance of conflict in a play—an early stage in the development of drama.

Above: John Briant bell, now in Hertford Museum.

Above: William Caffyn, a Hertford barber, who played cricket for Surrey and England. This print was dated 1852. He eventually emigrated to Australia to teach the inhabitants cricket!

Below: Hertford cricket team of 1889.

Left: Mr F. Walter Taylor, the muffin man, pictured in 1922.

Right: Mr T. R. Andrews (1839-1928) founder of the museum, and its first curator.

130

Labourers' SICK CLUB

Take Notice:

All Persons willing to Subscribe to a *SICK CLUB*, are recommended to have their names put down immediately, by *Mr. Woodhouse*, Surgeon, St. Andrew's St. Hertford.

Further information may be obtained by application to the Guardian or Guardians of each Parish in this Union.

TERMS OF SUBSCRIPTION,

(Payable in Advance.)

	QUARTERLY	FOR MAY AND JUNE 1836
For each Man	1 0	0 8
For each single Woman	0 9	0 6
For each Married Couple	1 6	1 0
For each Child under Sixteen Years old	0 6	0 4
For each Male or Female Servant whose Wages are between £5. and £10.	1 6	1 0
A whole Family in no case to exceed	2 6	1 8

All Persons subscribing as above, will receive Medical and Surgical Attendance of every kind (Midwifery and Trusses excepted) on their own application to Mr. Woodhouse. Vaccination is included.

All Persons who do not join this Club immediately must be prepared to pay their own Doctor's Bill in case of Sickness, with the exception of those who are Paupers.

☞ *The Board of Guardians will take no part in the Club, except by recommending it.*

THOMAS SWORDER,
Clerk to the Guardians of the Hertford Union.

Hertford, April 18, 1836.

STAUGHTON, PRINTER, HERTFORD.

The Health Service had not been thought of in 1836.

Above left: Mr Philip Longmore (1799-1879), a dogged town clerk.

Below left: Dr John Tasker Evans (1803-1895) a mayor who fought for a barracks in the town.

Below right: Mr William Henry Norris (1856-1904) founder of the building firm which erected some of the town's important buildings.

Above right: Mr Thomas Garratt, of Sele Roller Mills.

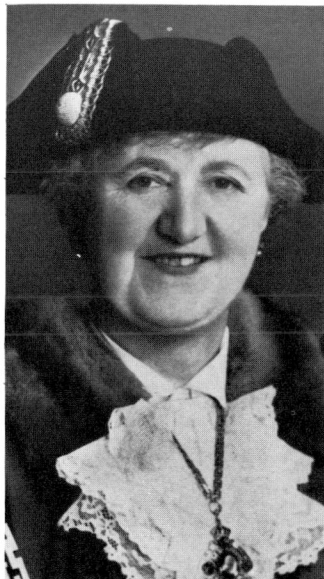

Above left: Ald Mrs Margaret Addis.

Above right: Ald Mrs M. H. Purkiss-Ginn.

Below left: Ald Alexander Purkiss Ginn, Freeman of the town, and
Mayor in 1900, 1901, 1911, 1919, and 1925.

Below right: Ald George Mansfield, Freeman of the town.

Centre right: Ald Mrs Winifred Brooks, first woman Freeman of the town as well as
first woman Mayor.

133

Fore Street at the turn of the century.

Yesterday's Town

Pargetting in Market Place and Fore Street.

The old Gladstone Arms, demolished to make way for the relief road.

The junction of Queens Road, Castle Street, and Parliament Square before the relief road.

Above: The Maidenhead Inn, in Maidenhead Street. Demolished and now the site of Woolworth's.

Below: The site of the Library.

The Old Coffee House Inn, demolished to make way for Burtons the Tailors in Maidenhead Street. It is now a shoe shop.

Above left: Honey Lane—an early picture.

Above right: Lord George Sanger's circus parades in Fore Street in the late 19th century.

Below: Cottages in Cowbridge—now gardens, demolished about 1890.

139

The Old Cross Keys Inn, next to the Corn Exchange.

......Faith in our future

What is Hertford's future? Many see it falling behind, being squeezed between the crushing concrete of surrounding new towns. Many are delighted at its old fashioned air, and fight to preserve it. But no town can hope to stand still and live.

Between the two schools of thought there is a great danger that the two sections of the town's motto "Pride in our past—Faith in our future" will become incompatible.

Those looking backwards have not been encouraged by some of the examples of modern architecture already in the town, but if there is to be a future in which to have any faith, some sort of progress will have to be made.

Hertford has lost a lot of its former pageantry and importance—the assizes and the borough council are but two examples—but it is still the county town, a position it has held for more than 1,000 years. There may be a future for the town as an increasingly necessary quiet retreat away from the high-powered, high rises of the new towns which are already bursting at the seams.

But the people who LIVE in the town must have the facilities to do just that. No one wants to live in a museum.

The multi-storey car park.

141

Left: The county fire brigade headquarters.

Right: Headquarters of "A" Division of the Hertfordshire Police.

The heart of Hertford?

Bibliography

Turnor's History of Hertford.
History of Hertford—Dr F. M. Page.
The Chronicles of Hertford Castle—H. C. Andrews.
Anglo-Saxon Chronicles.
A History of the English Church and People—Bede.
Cussans: History of Hertfordshire. Parts ix, x. Hundred of Hertford.
Dictionary of National Biography.
Domesday Book.
From Studio to Stage—Grossmith.
Hertford Corporation Records.
Chronica Majora—Matthew Paris.
Victoria County History of Herts.
Hertfordshire during the Great Civil War—Alfred Kingston.
Early English stages, 1300–1660. Vol. 1.—G. Wickham.
Stephen Austin of Hertford—James Moran.
The Brewing Industry of England—P. Mathias.
History of the River Lea—S. Hobday and F. S. Thacker.
Industrial Archaeology of Hertfordshire—W. Branch Johnson.
Is Hertford a Royal Borough?—pamphlet by Alfred Baker.
The Borough seal and arms, and the chaplain's badge—pamphlet by H. C. Andrews, and H. Bentley.
Place Names in Hertfordshire—English Place Name Society.
A Brief Record of Herts Yeomanry and Herts Artillery—Major A. L. P. Griffith.
Balls Park, Hertford—an illustrated booklet.
The Age of Chivalry—Arthur Bryant.
The First Hertford Quakers—Violet A. Rowe.
Hertford St Andrew—Canon R. H. Gill.
History of All Saints.
St Leonard's Church, Bengeo.

Appendix

The Canons approved at the Synod of Hertford 673. See pages 19 and 20.

Chapter 1.   That we all in common keep the Holy Day of Easter on the Sunday after the fourteenth moon of the first month.

Chapter 2.   That no bishop intrude into the diocese of another but be content with governing the people entrusted to him.

Chapter 3.   That it shall not be lawful for any bishop to disturb in any matter any monasteries dedicated to God nor to remove by force any of their possessions.

Chapter 4.   That the monks themselves shall not move from place to place, that is, from monastery to monastery unless sent forth by their own abbot but they are to continue in the obedience that they promised at the time of their profession.

Chapter 5.   That no cleric forsaking his own bishop shall wander about anywhere nor be received anywhere without commendatory letters from his own prelate. But if he is once received and will not return when summoned both the receiver and he who is received shall be under excommunication.

Chapter 6.   That bishops and clerics when travelling are to be content with the hospitality offered them and it shall not be lawful for any one of them to perform any priestly functions without the permission of the bishop in whose diocese he is known to be.

Chapter 7.   That the Synod shall be held twice a year but because various causes hindered this it was approved by all that we should meet once a year on 1st August at a place which is called Clofesho.

Chapter 8.   That no bishop through ambition shall set himself above another but all are to observe the time and order of their consecration.

Chapter 9.   The ninth chapter was discussed in common. 'That more bishops should be made as the number of the faithful increased.' But we passed over this matter for the present.

Chapter 10.   Relating to marriages. 'That nothing but lawful wedlock be allowed to anyone. No one shall commit incest and no one shall leave his own wife unless on account of fornication, as the Holy Gospel teaches. And if anyone divorce his own wife joined to him by lawful wedlock he shall take no other if he wishes truly to be a Christian, but remain as he is or be reconciled with his own wife.'

Index

A

Abel Smith Family 56, 57
Abel Smith School 108
Adam, James 91
Adams Family 77
Adams, John Carter 78
Addis Ltd. 79
Addis, Mrs Robert 127
Alfred, King 23, 24
All Saints Church 13, 24, 48, 55, 56, 79, 116, 117, 125, 128
All Saints Infants School 108
Andrews, R. T. 127
Andrews, Ald W. F. 127
Angel, The 126
Angles 23
Anglo-Saxon Chronicles 23
ARP 117
Artillery 116, 117
Ashbourne Ditch 24
Association of Gentlemen 116
Ashton, William 89
Athelstan 24
Austin, Stephen 78, 108

B

Baker, Herbert 125
Baker, Sir William 68
Baker, William, Technical School 68
Balfour, Arthur James 127
Ball, John 41
Balls Park 36, 69
Balls Park College of Education 70
Balle, Simon de 36, 69
Balle, Simon, School 107
Baptist Church 58
Barclays Bank 77, 126
Barnardo's, Dr 68
Battell, Dionisia 56
Bayford, Manor of 35
Bayfordbury 68
Bayley Hall 107
Bedfordshire Regiment 116
Belgae 14
Bell, The, later Salisbury Arms 115, 126
Bengeo 13, 14, 20
Bengeo C of E School 108
Benington Castle 34
Berwick, Treaty of 41
Bibliography 144
Bigg, Rachael 91
Blackbirds, The 77, 126
Black Lyon, The 126
Blanche 41
Blue Coats 107
Boleyn, Anne 47
Borough Council 92
Brazier, H. Ltd 79
Briant, John 79, 125
Bricha 67
Brickendonbury 67
Brickendonbury, hoard 14
Bridgeman, Charles 56
British & Foreign Schools Society 108
Bronze Age Urn 13
Brooks, Ald Percy 127
Brooks, Mrs Winifred 127
Bruce, David 41
Buckingham, Duke of 42
Bull, The 126
Burt, Cpl A. 117
Byde family 56, 69

C

Cage, The 91
Caesar, Sir Charles 90
Calvinist Independent Chapel 58
Canterbury, Archbishop of 19
Castle 20, 25, 33
Catherine 41
Catherine Wheel, The 126
Caxton 78
Cecil, see Salisbury
Chalice, Elizabethan 89
Charles I 49, 67, 90
Charles II 90
Charters 41, 48, 89, 90
Chauncey, Sir Henry 92
Chequers, The 77, 91, 126
Christ Church 57
Christ's Hospital School 57, 107
Christmas Tree 68
Chronicle of Bermondsey Priory 55
Churchill, Odette 68
Cockbush Field 115
Comley, W. J. 56
Congregational Church 57
Constance 41
Cornbury, Viscount 116
Corn drier, Roman 14
Corn Exchange 24, 56, 90, 92
County of Hertford 68
County Hall 13, 79
County Hospital 92
Cowbridge House 58
Cowper family 49, 56, 57, 67, 68, 90, 116, 126
Cowper Memorial School 108
Cox, Edward 67
Creaseys of Hertford 79
Cressant, The 126
Crimean War 116
Cromwell 115
Cross Keys, The 126

D

Dalton, Joseph 90
Dame School 108
Danelaw 23
Danes 23
Dauphin, of France, Louis 34
Denny, Sir Anthony 47, 55, 69
Desborough, Lady 68
de Tany 55
Dicker Mill 25, 79
Dimsdale Arms 24, 126
Dimsdale, Baron 125
Dimsdale, Sir John 107
Dodderidge, F. W. 127
Domesday Book 25
Downshire, Marquess of 67
Dragoons, The First 116
Duncombe Arms 126
Duncombe, Thomas Slingsby 126
Dye's Dipping Place 24, 77

E

East Herts District Council 92
East Herts Hospital 69, 92
East India Company 67, 69, 108
Ebenezer Strict Baptist Chapel 58
Edgar 24, 115
Edward I 35
Edward II 36
Edward III 41
Edward IV 42, 47
Edward VI 48
Edward the Elder 24
Elections 91
Elizabeth I 47, 48
Elizabeth, Queen Mother 147
Elizabeth Woodville, Queen 42, 47
Elizabeth of York, Queen 42
Ermine Street 14, 23
Essendon, Manor of 35
Evans, Dr John 116

F

Fairfax, General 115
Falcon, The 126
Fanshawe family 56, 69
Fanshaw, Thomas 89
Faudel-Phillips, Sir George 70, 127
Faudel-Phillips, Sir Benjamin 70
Faudel-Phillips, Sir Lionel 70
Finch, Sir John 126
Fitz Emme 34
Fitz Walter 34
Fitz Wiger 34
Fox, George 57
Foxholes Farm 14

G

Gallows Hill 91
Gaols 35, 90
George, The 126
Gilpin, the Rev. Bernard 58
Glove, The 126
Godarvil, Walter de 34
Goldings 68
Gospel Hall 58
Grammar School 107
Green Coat School 108
Green Dragon, The 126
Grindecobbe, John 41
Gunnora 34
Guthrum 23
Guyse, John 57

H

Haesten 23
Haileybury College 67, 78, 108
Hale, Richard 107
Hale, Richard – school 107
Harrington, Sir William 49, 67
Harold I 69
Harrison, Edward 69
Harrison, George 69
Harrison, Sir John 55, 69, 90
Hatfield Polytechnic 68
Hartford, Connecticut 126
Hartham 126
Heenan, Cardinal 19
Henry I 33
Henry II 33
Henry III 34, 35
Henry IV 41
Henry V 42
Henry VI 42
Henry VII 42, 78
Henry VIII 47
Hertford College Youths Society of Change Ringers 125
Hertford Company of Players 57
Hertford Dramatic and Operatic Society 128
Hertfordshire Mercury 19, 78
Hertfordshire Regiment 116, 127
Hertingfordbury 14, 20, 49, 108
High Steward 89
Hoggshills, The 126
Hollybush School 108
Holy Trinity Church 56, 57
Home Guard 117
Honor 42, 89
Hope Breweries 78
Horseshoes, The 126
Horns Mill 79
Hunger, John 56

I

Ice Ages 13
Immaculate Conception & St Joseph,
    Church of 20, 58
Imperial Service College 108
Ingestre, Lord 91
Innes, John, Horticultural Institute ... 68
International Gas Co 78
Isabella, Queen 36
Isabella, Princess 41

J

James I 48, 49
James I of Scotland 42
Joan of Navarre, Queen 42
John I 34
John, King of France 41, 56
John of Gaunt 41

K

Katherine of Aragon 47
Katherine, Queen 42
Kelyng, John 90
Kings Arms, The 126
Kings Head, The 13, 126
Kings Mead 90, 126
Kit Kat Portraits 68
Kneller, Sir Godfrey 68

L

Labour-in-Vain, The 126
Leahoe House 79
Leake, Martin 116
Lee, Godfrey de la 36
Lee, River 13, 23, 33, 36, 48, 77
Levellers, The 115
Library 92
Lilburn 115
Limesy, Ralph de 25
Lombard House 92
Lonchamps, William 33
Longmore, John 117
Longmore, Philip 67, 92
Longmore, Philip Raynsford 127
Lorynge, the Rev 48
Luscombe, Dr 67
Lydgate, John 128

M

Mace 89, 90
Mahon, Lord 91
Maidenhead, The 126
Maidenhead Street 24, 57
Malaysian Rubber Producers
    Research Association 68
Mangrove Road 14
Manisty, William 48
Mansfield, George 127
Margaret of Anjou 42
Margaret, Queen 35
Mary I 47, 48
Mary, Queen of Scots 48
Matreyvers, the Rev. John 48
Matilda 33
Maud, Princess 25
McMullens of Hertford 78, 79
McMullen, Alexander Peter 67
Meads 41, 49
Messenger, Dr. E. 19
Methodist Church 58
Militia 116
Mill Bridge 24, 79, 127
Millmead School 108
Montfitchet, Richard de 34
More, Sir Thomas 47
Morgan family 67
Morgan's Walk School 108
Municipal Corporations Act 92
Museum 92
Mylne, William Chadwell 79

N

Naked Boy, The 126
National Agricultural
    Advisory Service 68
National School 108
Nayler, James 57
New River 79
Newton, Gabriel 108
Noble, The Rev. Thomas 48
Norden, John 48
North Met. Electric Power &
    Distribution Co., Ltd. 78

O

Observer Corps 117
Old Coffee House 126
Old Cross 24

P

Panshanger House 68
Palmer, Andrew 90
Parker, W. F. 69
Paris, Matthew 35
Parliament at Hertford 48
Paper Mill 78
Pearson, Sir Edward 67, 92, 127
Pearson, George 67
Pembrok, Earl of 35
Permanite Ltd. 79
Philip Augustus, French King 33
Philip IV of France 35
Plague, The 48
Plymouth Brethren 58
Powell, Chief Justice 91
Prince's Arms, The 126
Priory, The 25, 35, 55, 69
Privy Council 48
Puller, Isaac 90
Purkiss Ginn, Alex 19, 127
Purkiss-Ginn, Mrs. M. H. 127
Pynere, Richard 57

Q

Queens Hill bowl 14
Queen Mother,
    Queen Elizabeth 20, 70, 117
Quaker Meeting House 57

R

Ragged School 58
Railways 78
Ram Inn 77
Redd Lion 126
Reeve 24
Repton 68
Revels Hall 56
Rib, River 55
Richard I 33
Richard II 41
Richard III 42
Robert III of Scotland 42
Romans 14
Roman Catholic School 108
Rose, The 126

S

St Albans Abbey 25
St Andrew Church 48, 55, 56, 57
St Andrew Church – School 108
St John's Church 55
St Leonard's Church 55, 56
St Mary the Great 25, 55
St Mary the Less Church ... 24, 25, 55
St Mary's Church, Tonwell 55
St Nicholas Church 24, 25, 55
St Joseph's Convent School 108
Salisbury Arms 126
Salisbury family 20, 49, 67, 89
Salvation Army 58
Say, Sir Robert 35
Saxons 14, 23, 77
Sele Farm 13, 108
Sele Roller Mills 78, 79
Sessions House 89, 91
Seymour, Jane 47

Shipp Inn, The 91
Shire Hall 24, 79
Smith, Robert 57, 68
Sovereign House 80
Special Operations Executive
    European Theatre of War 68
Spencer, Robert 89
Star Chamber 48
Stephen of Blois 33
Straw plaiting 78
Stone Age Beaker 13
Stone, John 126
Stone, Samuel 48, 126
Swan, The 126
Sweeting, Henry 57
Sword, borough 90
Synod of Hertford 673 .... 19, 144

T

Tate, John, paper mill 78
Taylor, Christopher 108
Templars, The 36
Territorials 116, 117
Thames, River 13
Thany, Peter de 35
Theodore of Tarsus 19
Thomas Lord Cromwell 47
Three Tuns, The 126
Tonson, Jacob 68
Townshend family 69, 70
Tudor, Sir Owen 42
Turnor, William 90
Tyler, Wat 41

U

United Reformed Church 57

V

V Rockets 117
Valances, William de 35
Valoignes, Peter 33, 56
Valoignes, Roger 33, 56
Volunteers 116

W

War Memorial 92
Ware 13, 23, 25, 34, 49, 77
Ware Park 56, 69
Ware Road pottery 14
Wash, The 14, 33, 91
Water Hall Farm 13
Watling Street 23
Webb, Sir Aston 92
Webb & Co. 79
Wellington, Duke of 127
Wenham, Jane 91
Wesley, John 58
Westall, Richard 70, 127
Westall, William 127
Westreete, John de 36
Whig Reform Bill 90, 91
White Hart, The 126
Whitenail, Thomas 91
William I 24, 33, 89
William II 24, 33
Willis, Thomas 55
Willis, "Father" 56
Willis, Richard 69
Willis, Sir Thomas 69
Wool 77
Woolpack, The 77, 91
Worde, Wynkyn de 78
Wren, Ald. Josiah 89

Y

Yeomanry, Herts 116, 117
Young, 2nd Lt., F. E. 117

Z

Zeppelin raids 117

Hertfordshire Agricultural Show at Redbourn, May 1975: Her Majesty Queen Elizabeth the Queen Mother accepts the No 1 presentation copy of the First Edition of *The Book of Hertford* from author Cyril Heath and (behind him) publisher Clive Birch. Mr G. D. Wentworth-Stanley, the Show President, looks on.

147

The endpapers show: Speed's Map of Hertford, printed in 1610 showing the Royal Palace of Hertford before it was demolished in the 17th Century. It is also the only representation of the two Market Crosses, and the Saxon Church of St. Nicholas.

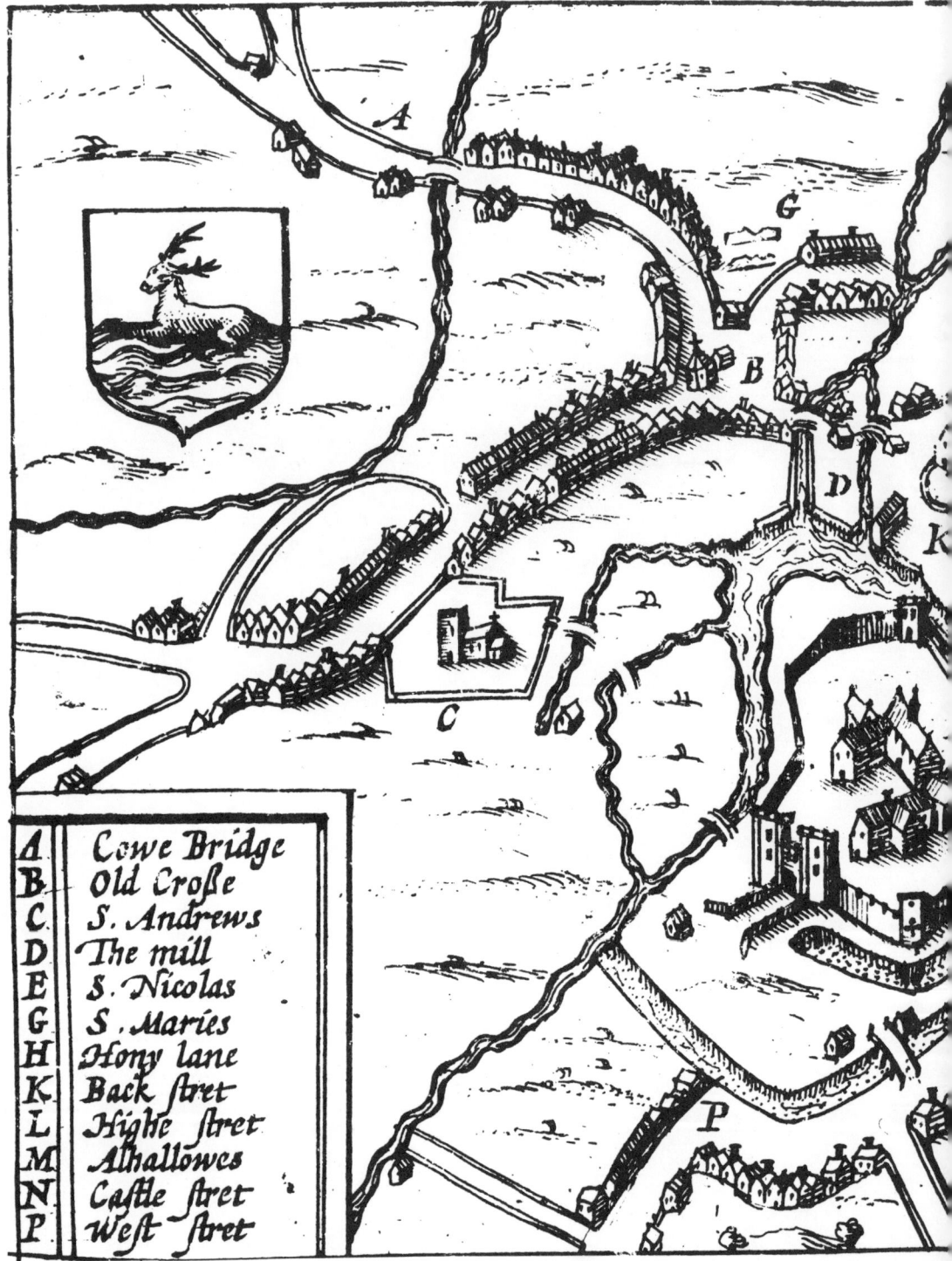

A	Cowe Bridge
B	Old Croſſe
C	S. Andrews
D	The mill
E	S. Nicolas
G	S. Maries
H	Hony lane
K	Back ſtret
L	Highe ſtret
M	Alhallowes
N	Caſtle ſtret
P	Weſt ſtret

SPEED'S MAP OF HERTFORD, PRINTED IN 1610.

This is the only picture of the Royal Palace of Hertford
only representation of the two Market Crosses and the S